The Jack Davis Sketchbook of Untold Spooky Ghost Stories

BY JOSEPH PFEIFFER

ASYLUM
PUBLICATIONS, INC.

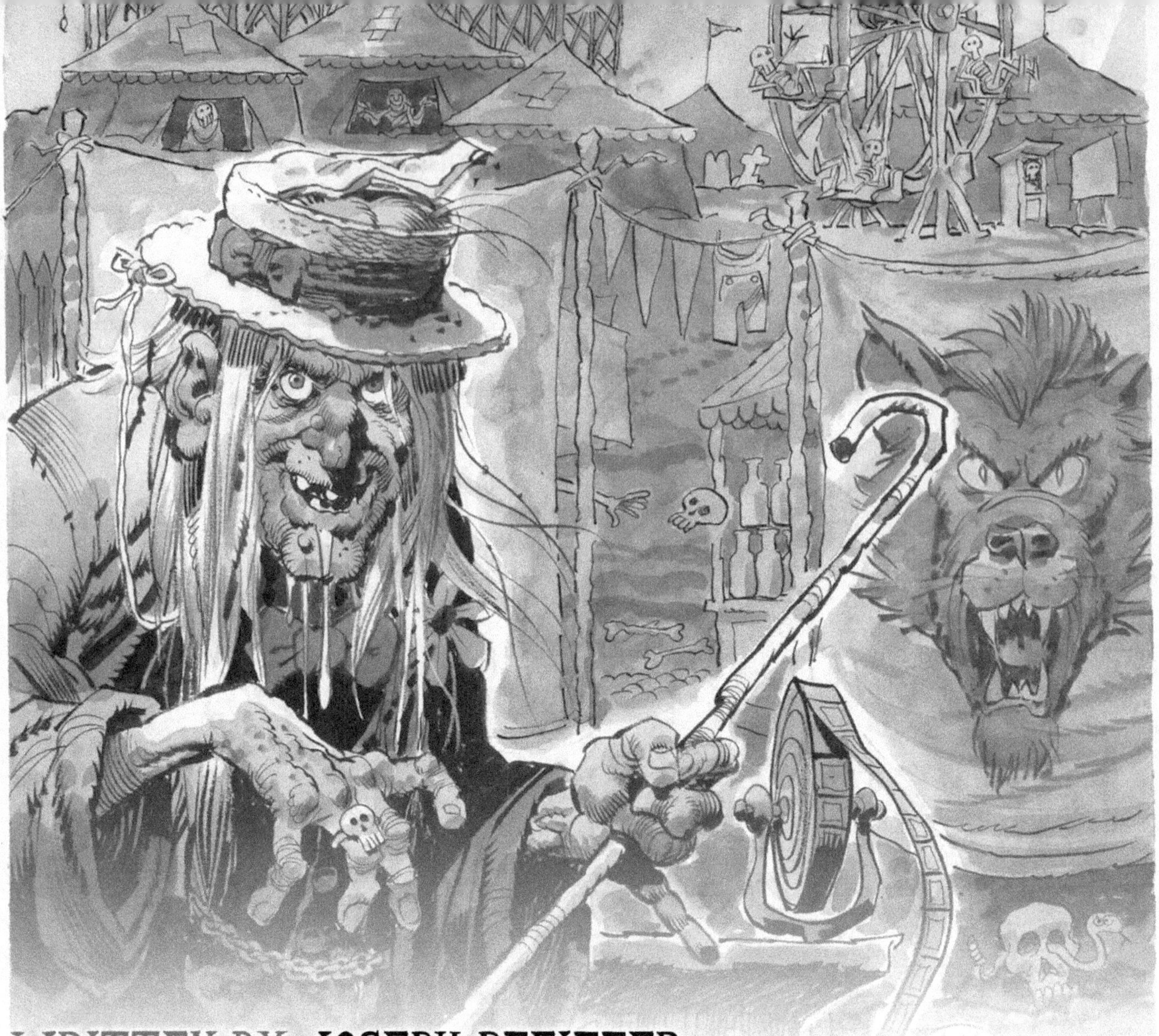

WRITTEN BY **JOSEPH PFEIFFER**
ARTWORK BY **JACK DAVIS**
COMPILED AND DESIGNED BY **JOSEPH PFEIFFER**
EDITED BY **JOSHUA WERNER & PAUL BURKE**

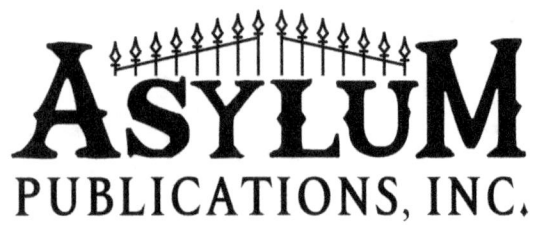

Distributed by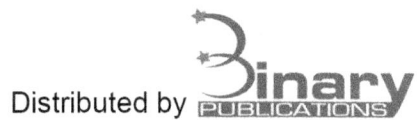

CEO AND EDITOR IN CHIEF **PAUL BURKE**
CREATIVE DIRECTOR **JOSHUA WERNER**

ISBN: 978-1-7363197-2-7
The Jack Davis Sketchbook of Untold Spooky Ghost Stories™. Published by Asylum Publications, Inc.™ © 2022 by Joseph Pfeiffer. Asylum Pulications, Inc. logo TM 2019. All rights reserved. No portion of this publication may be reproduced or transmitted, in any form by any means, without written consent from the Publisher, except for any small excerpts for the purpose of review. For further information regarding custom photo/art books, ordering wholesale, or other inquiries, please write to asylumpublications75@gmail.com.

Of all the beautifully finished illustrations Jack kept in his studio, a dusty old cardboard box containing his pencil sketches were his favorite. As Jack put it, "my final artwork represents the technical talents of creating the illustration, but I find the creative talents are best pictured in my pencil sketches".

In this book we have shared some of the many spooky sketches Jack drew over his 60-year career entertaining us in EC comics, Humbug, Mad Magazine, Topps trading cards, movie posters, Time and TV Guide covers, record albums, game boards and more. Best of all Jack will be remembered for his kind heart and Impish smile.

This sketch book is a testament to that talent. Enjoy!

As a boy, Jack loved to draw pictures and sometimes make up stories around each drawing, so it should be no surprise that his favorite subject as a student was Art Class.

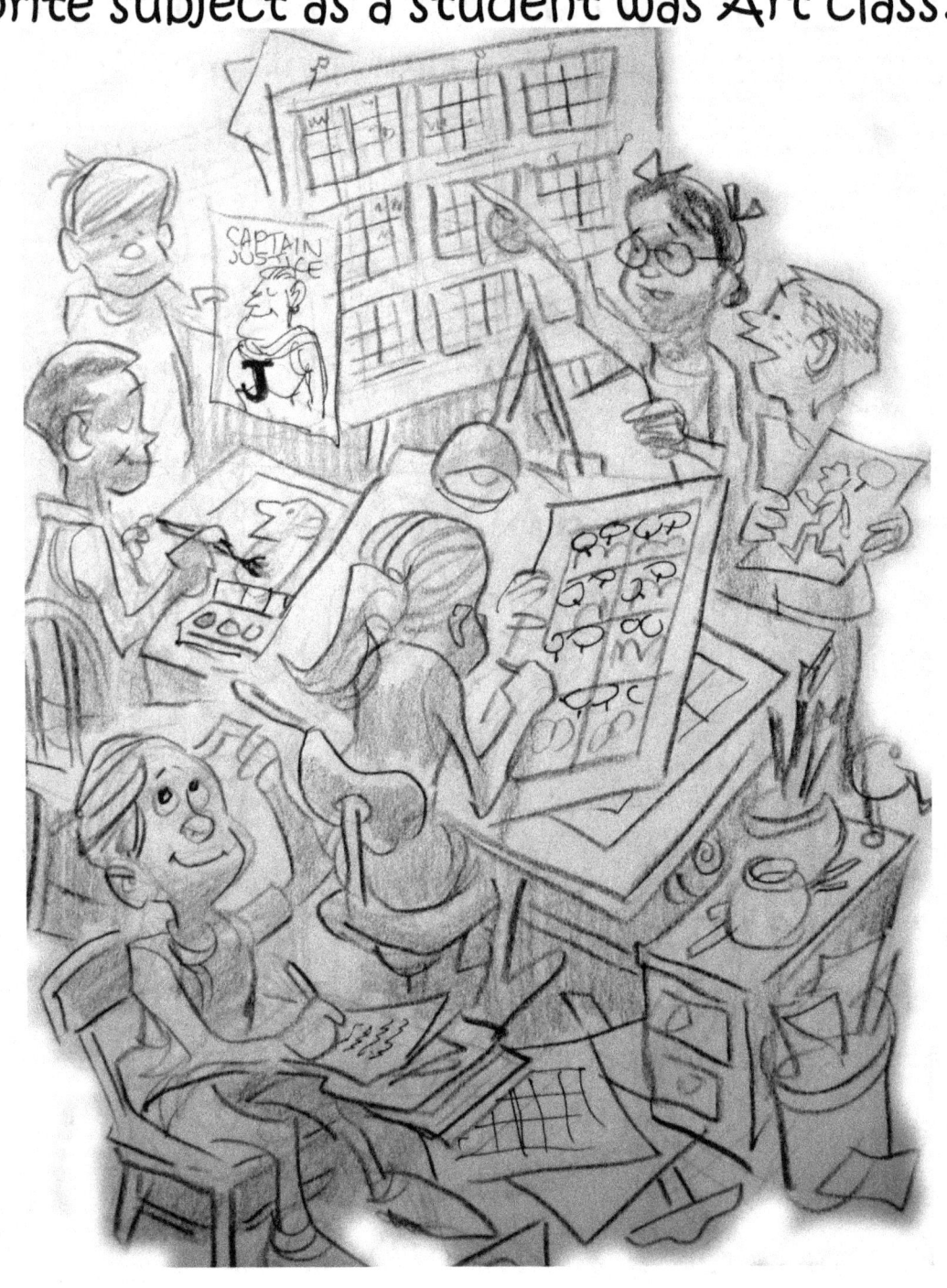

There was just one problem. Young Jack had an imagination that was off the charts. So much so that it was hard for him to stay focused on one thing at a time. If there had been a device to see what was going on in Jack's mind, I am sure it would have displayed a very busy place, a never-ending parade of new ideas marching all day long.

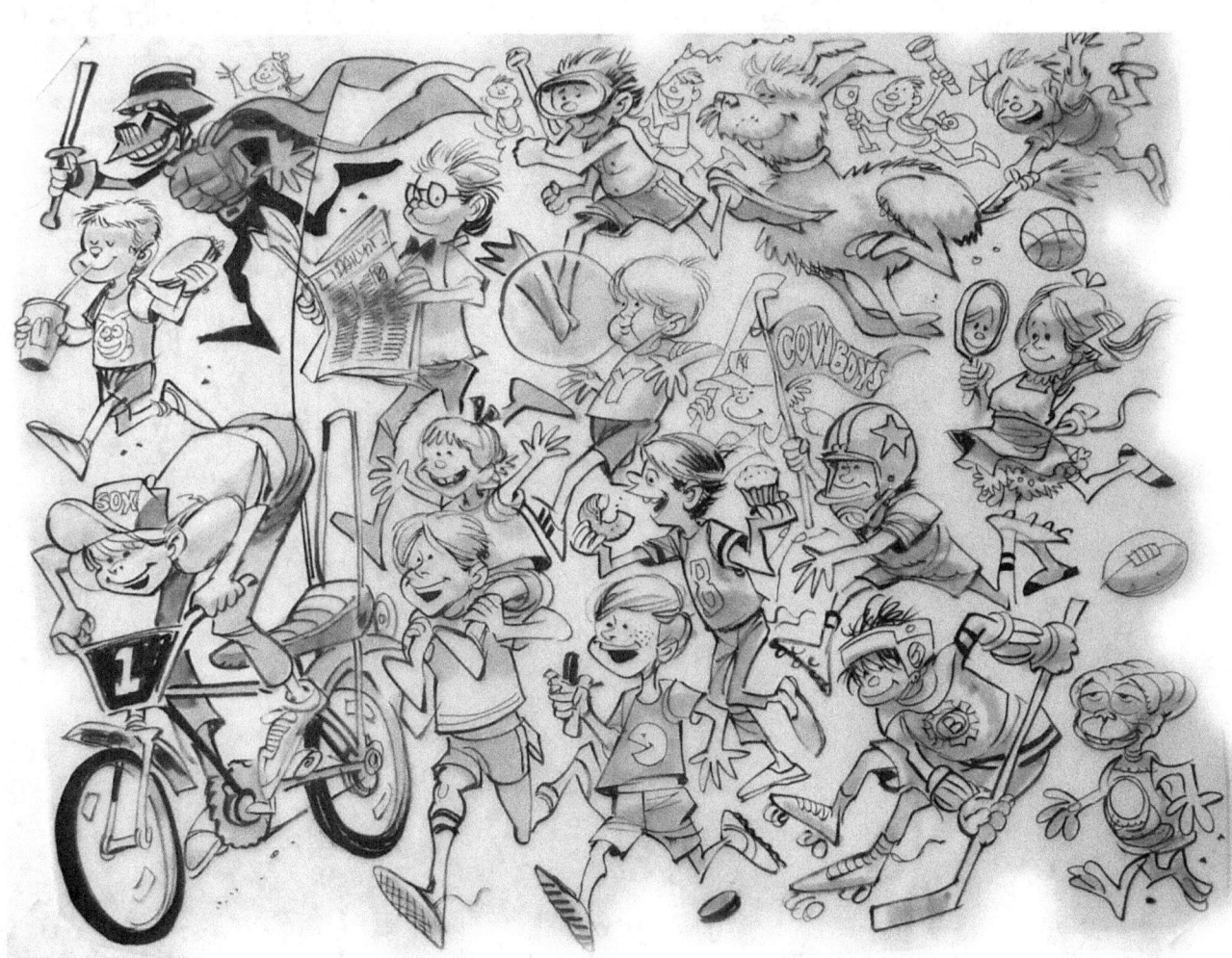

One of Jack's favorite things to draw were spooky scenes, so we decided to illustrate a book about the untold stories behind them. Too bad we never got the full story behind Jack's creative drawings.

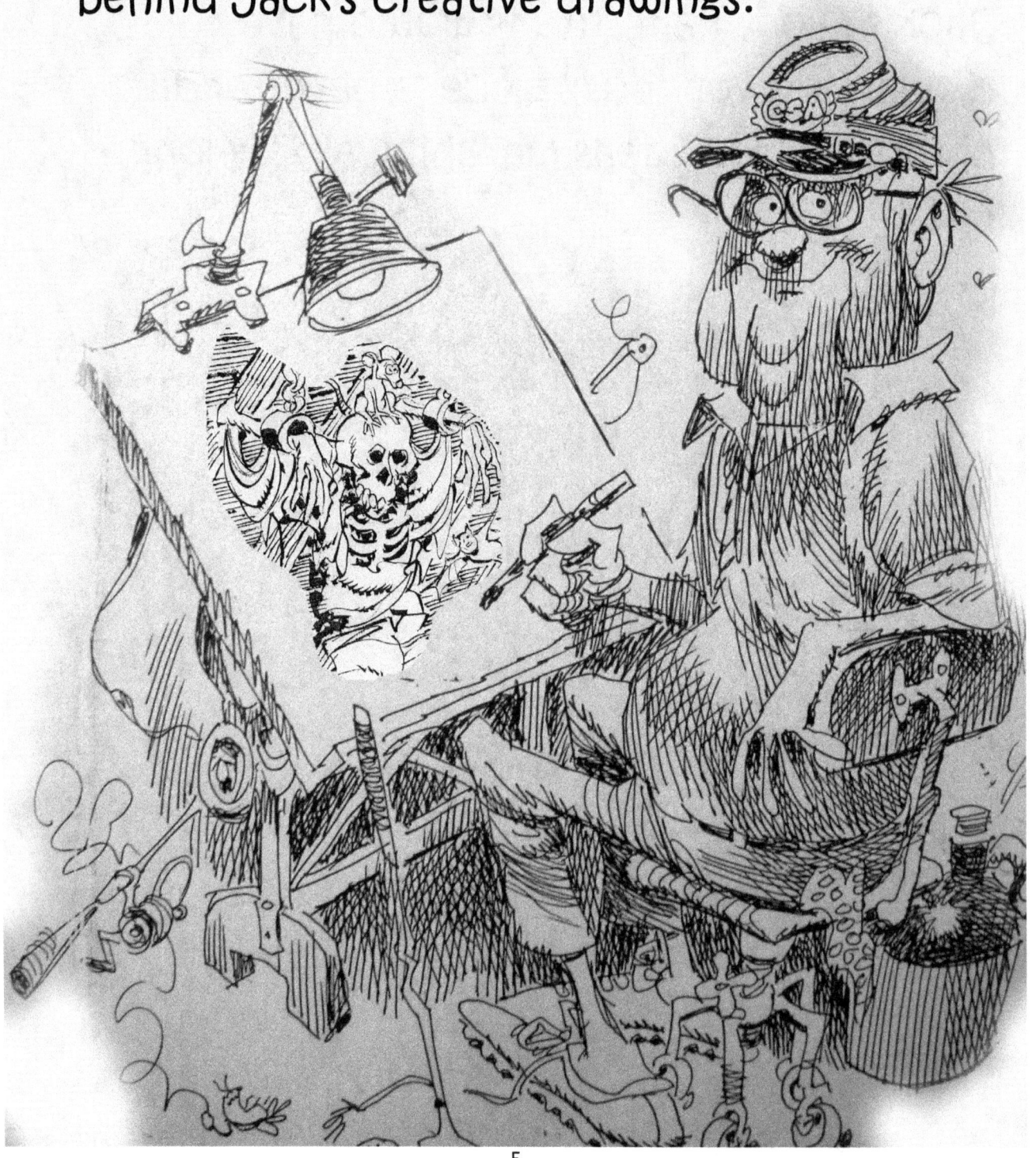

Jack's book starts with a sketch of two kids who were exploring a dusty old attic in an old abandoned house. Finding a strange book, they opened it, only to release the book's uninvited occupants who came floating off the pages behind them....

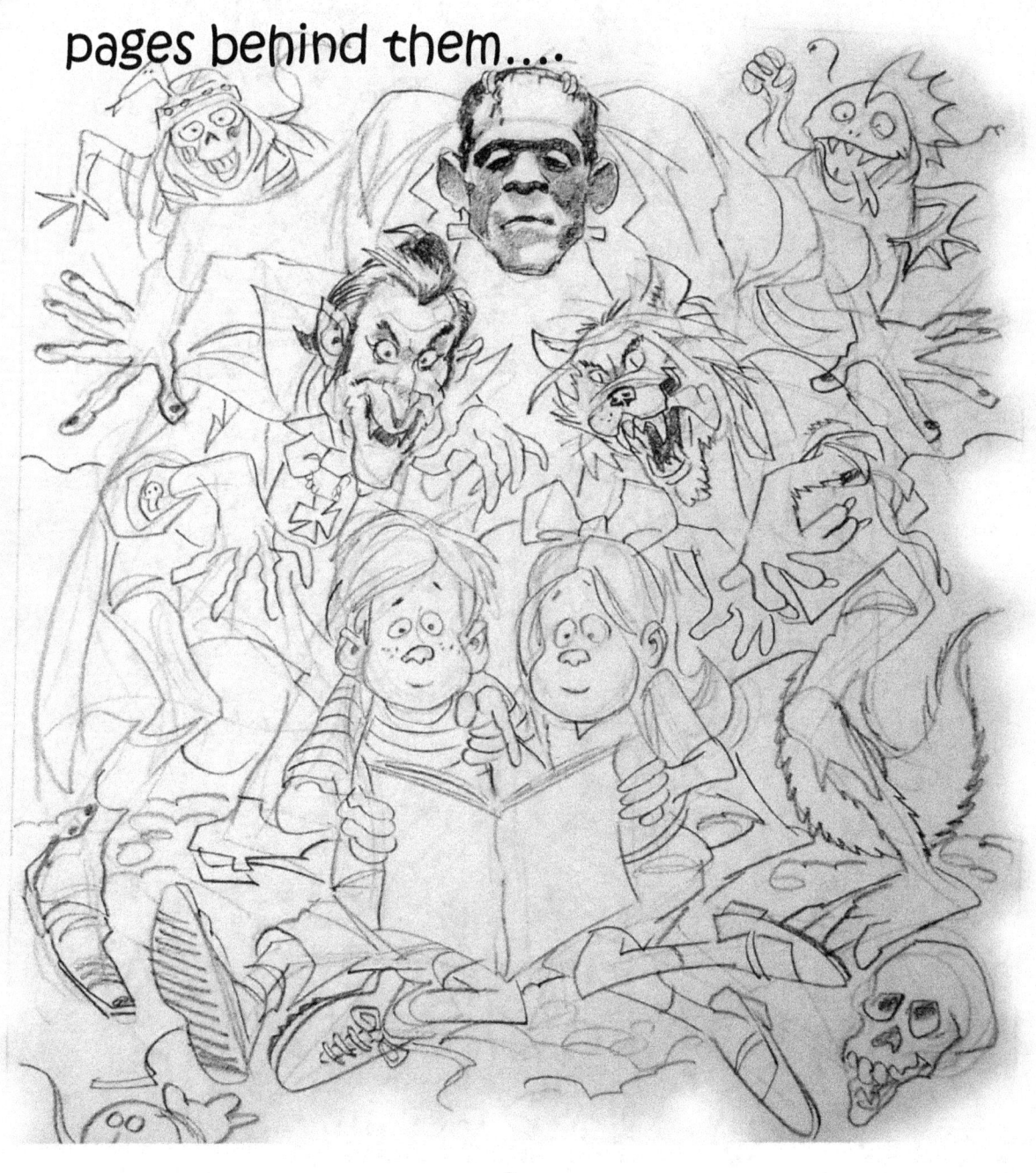

This next sketch pictured a haunted carnival that mysteriously appeared one windy October night at midnight. Even more unusual, was that everyone at the carnival appeared to be deceased.

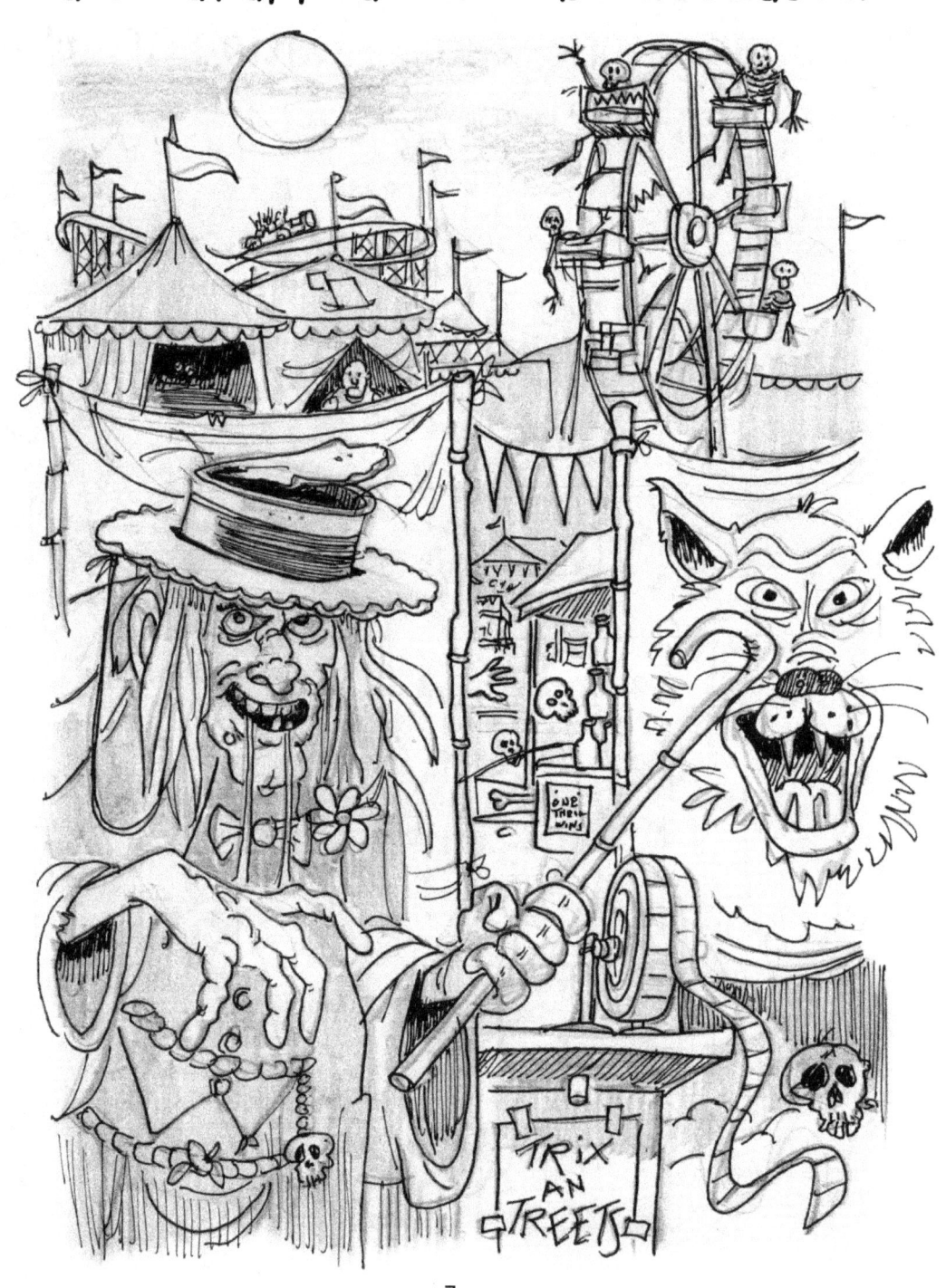

How about this sketch picturing a witch who brews a magic potion that conjures dead Pirates back to life along with hungry Alligators to be featured in a new action film…

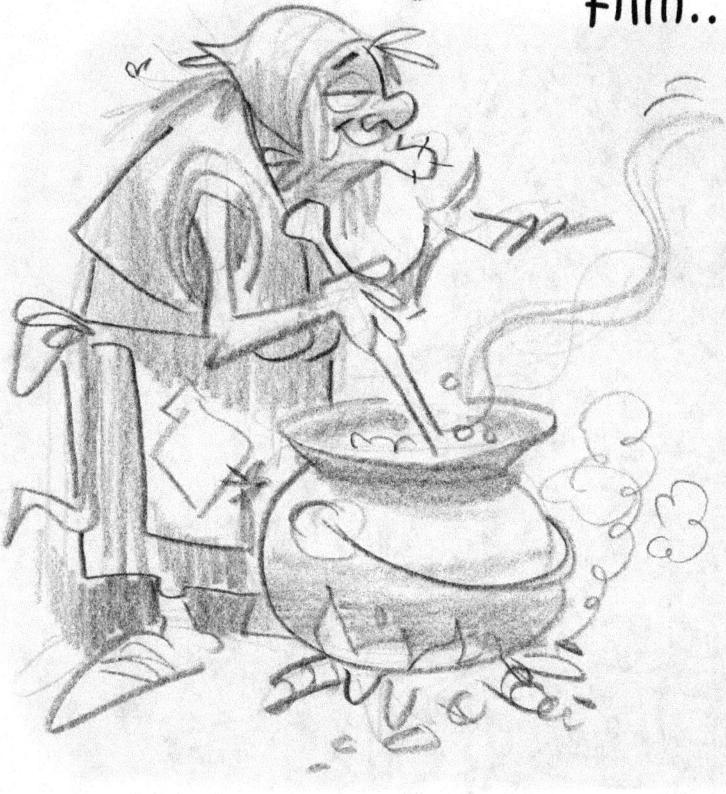

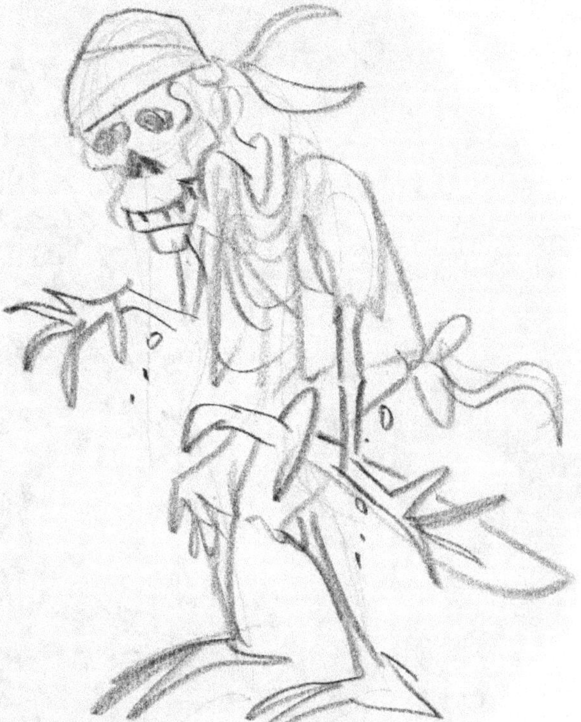

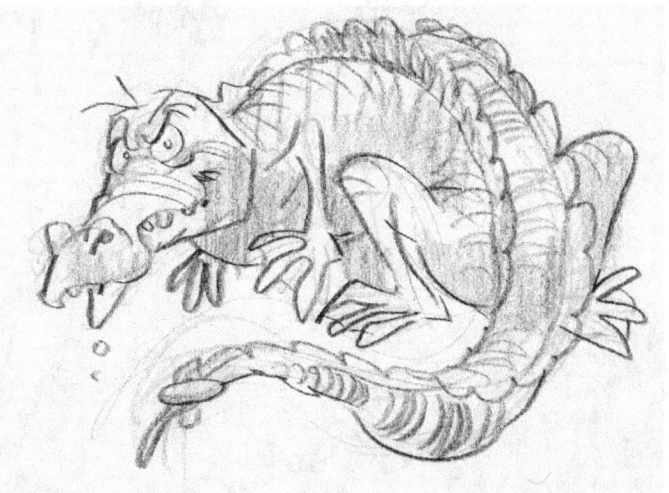

Entitled, "Gator-Nado"

Or maybe a sketch about a haunted house, but not your typical old haunted house. This one can *walk*, roaming the countryside each night looking for curious children to invite in.

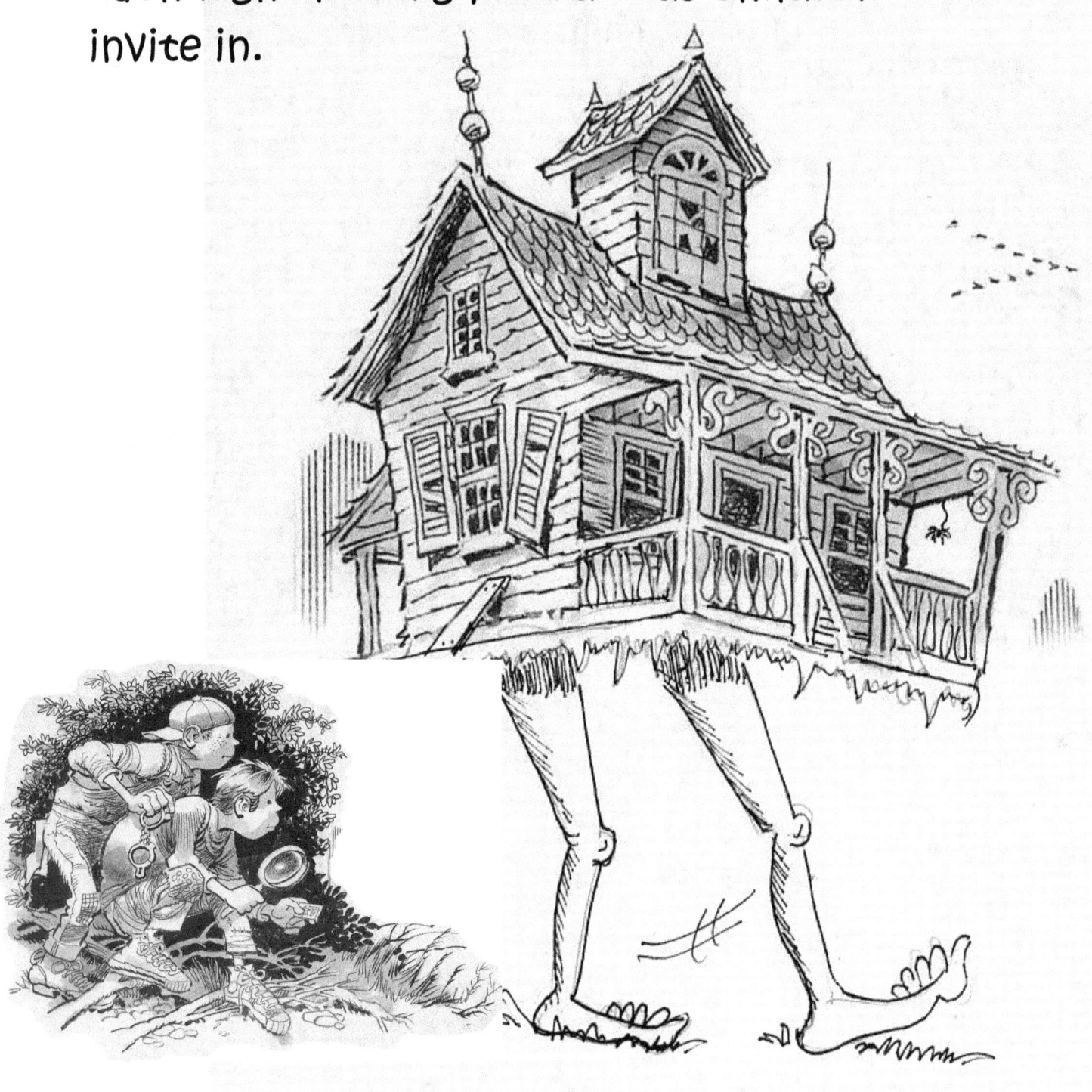

Then there is this sketch about a possessed bicycle that roamed the forest and would attract unsuspecting hunters to hop on and take a ride. Unfortunately, the bike would speed off and the riders would never be seen again, only their hats could be found.

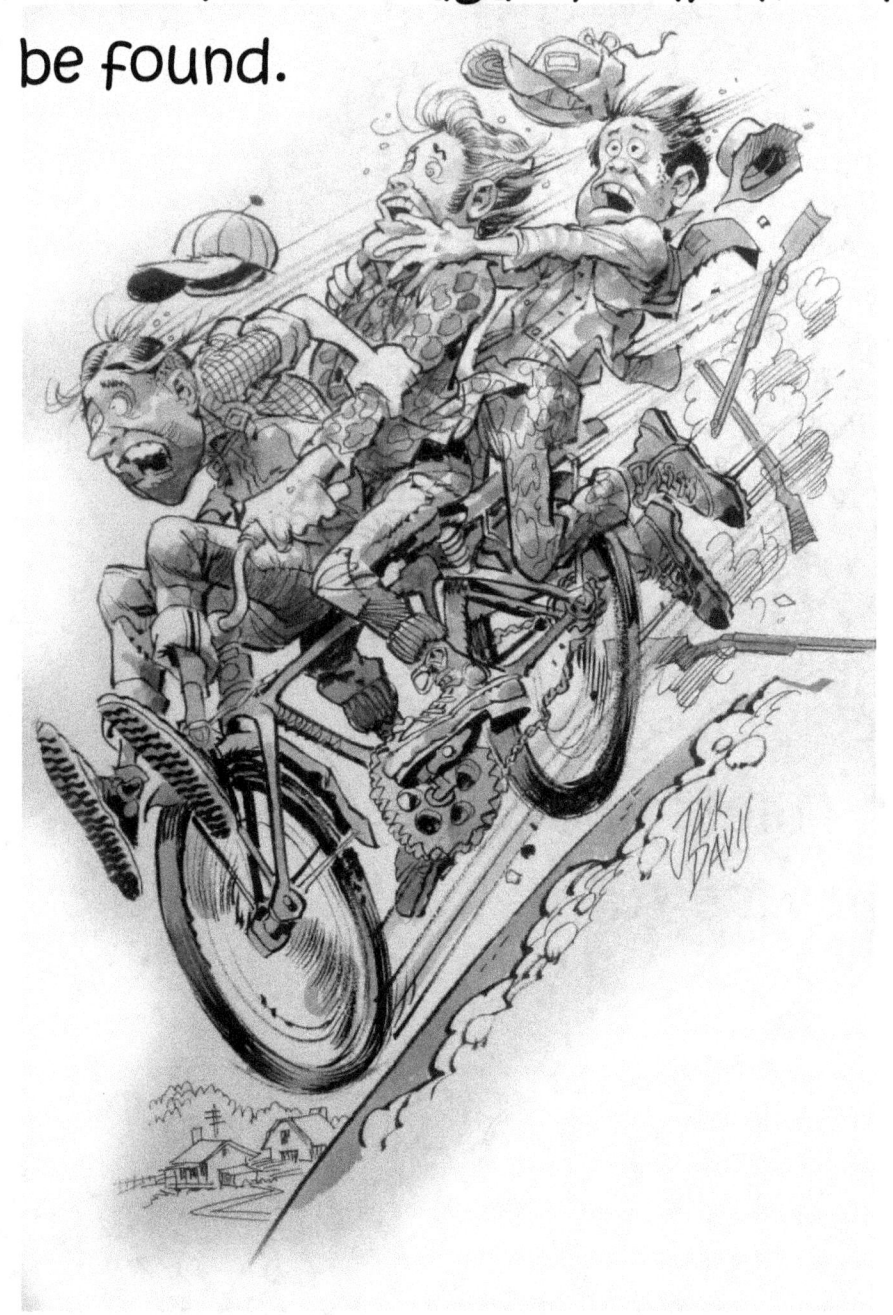

Or how about a sketch picturing a hungry freezer monster that lived in the basement of an old, abandoned house and would lure kids into the basement with tasty ice cream bars...

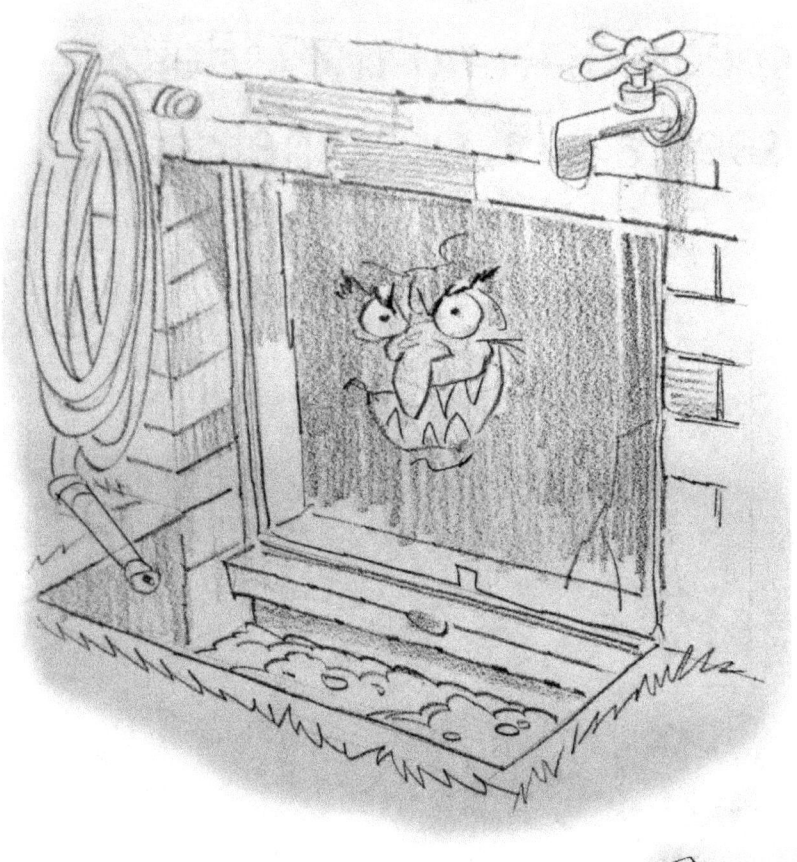

...then freeze the kids into ice statues.

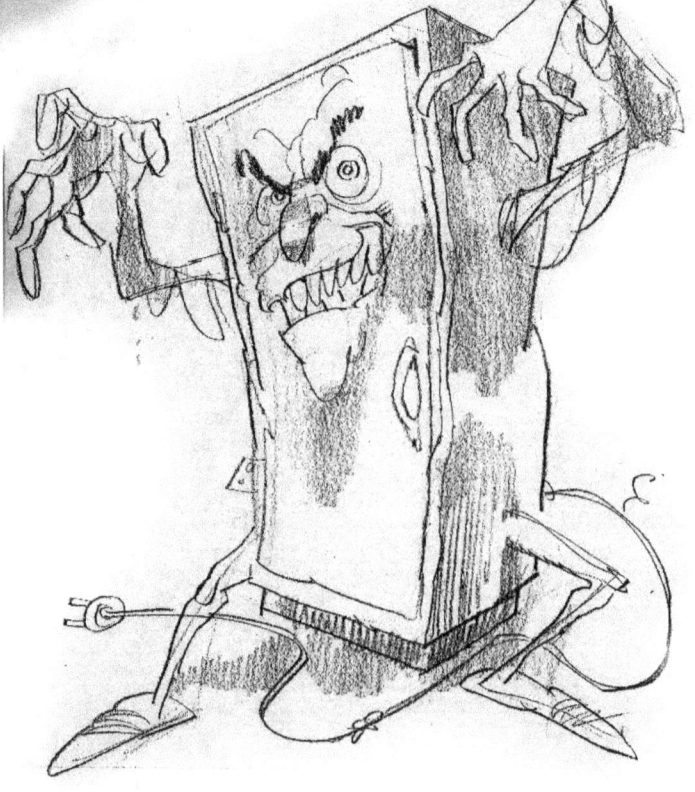

Here's another spooky sketch showing four strange singing brothers who would appear out of nowhere from the wilderness surprising unsuspecting campers sitting around a campfire. The four brothers seemed innocent enough and would offer to sing songs about frightening things that lived deep in the forest, then actually conjure up the creatures from their stories to join in the fun.

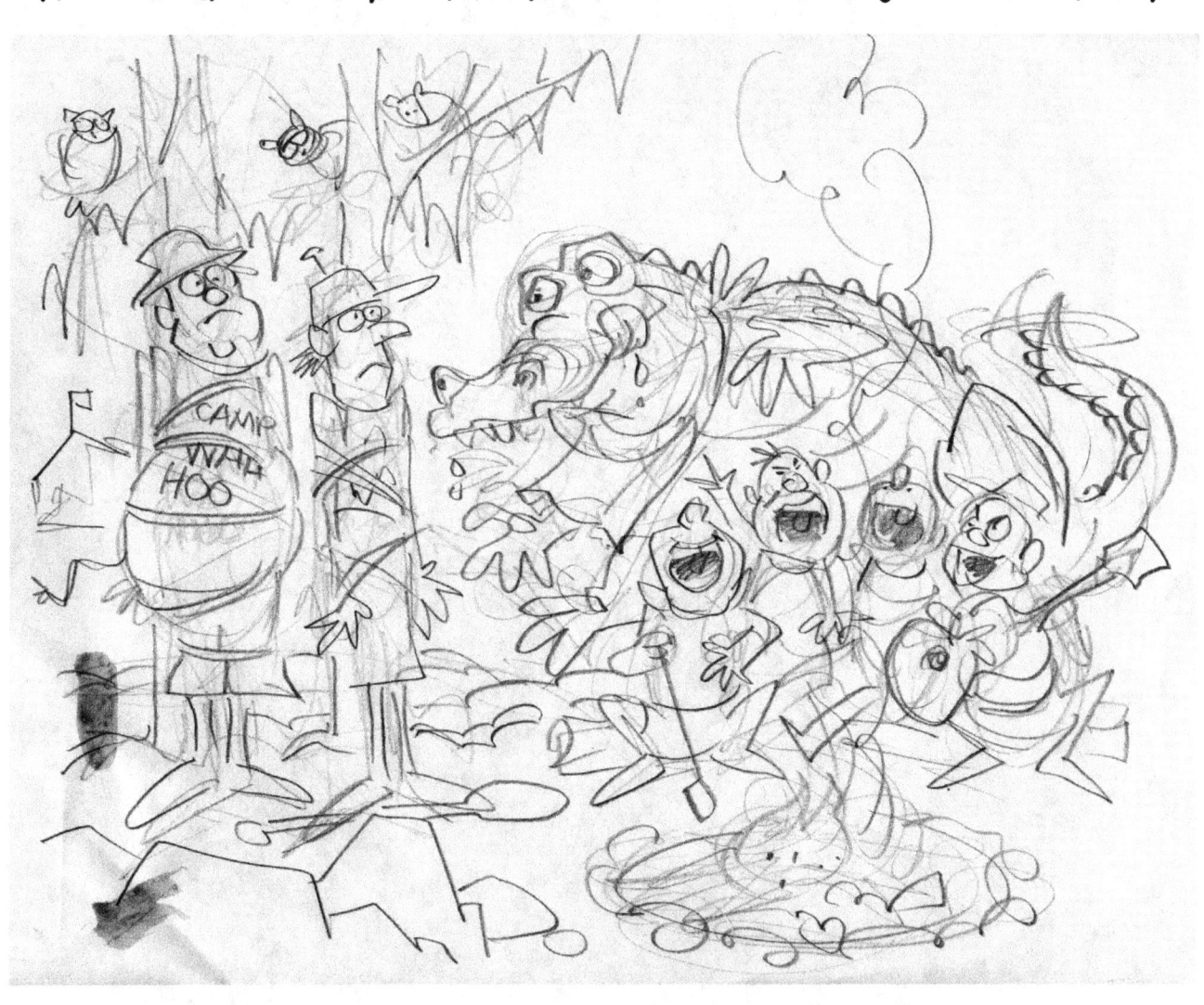

Another Frightening Sketch pictures a creepy dark Carnival Fortune teller Who Would transform Unsuspecting customers back to their childhood.

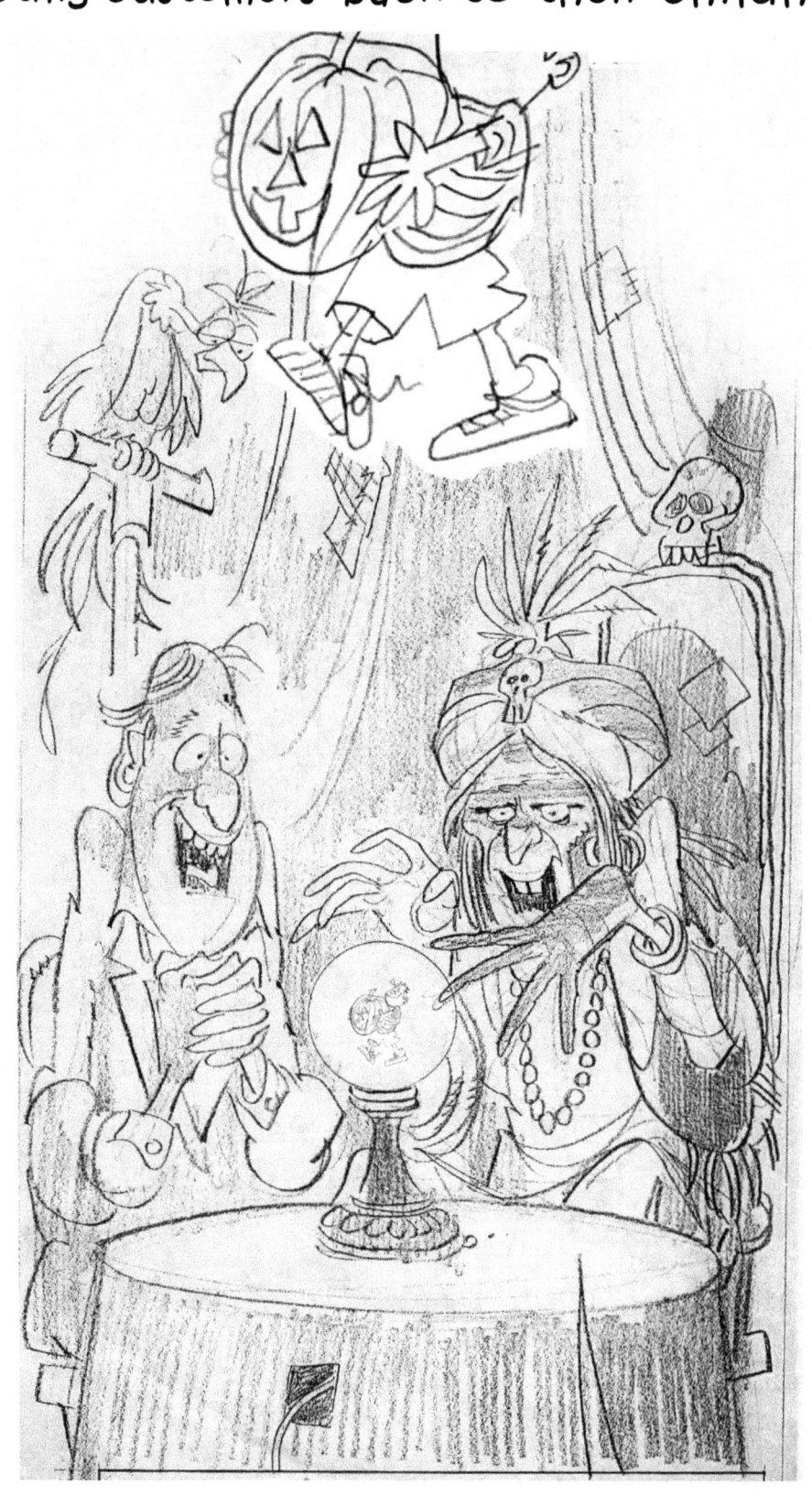

In this sketch a whacko Scientist offers a curious boy, who dropped by, a tour of his attic to show off a collection of other prior visitors who also dropped in and are now transformed into one of his many inventions.

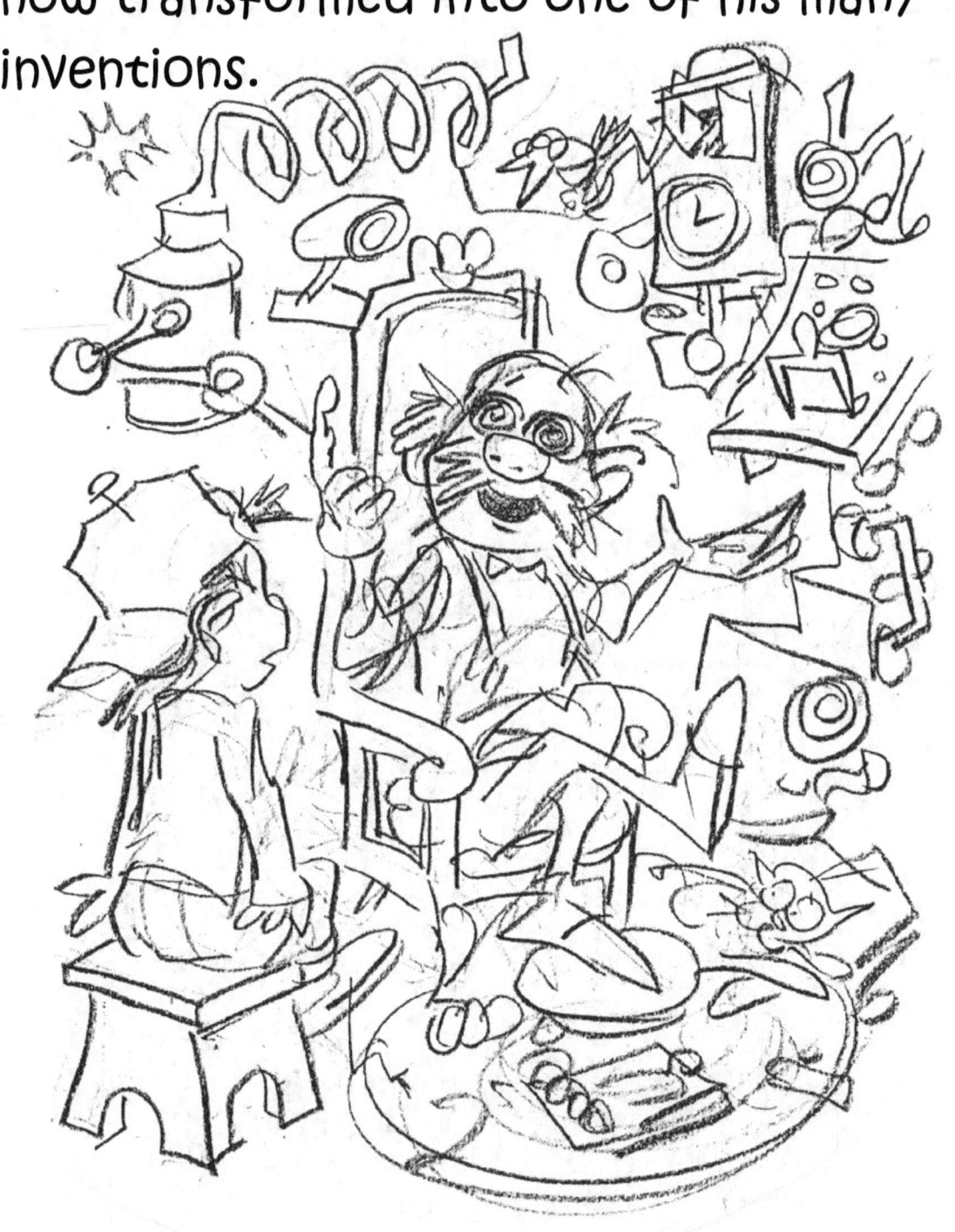

Many of us remember as a kid the days of going to summer camp with some reservations. This sketch pictures a camp where few kids never return, while the camp staff are just "Dying" to meet you. Come on in, there's room for one more.

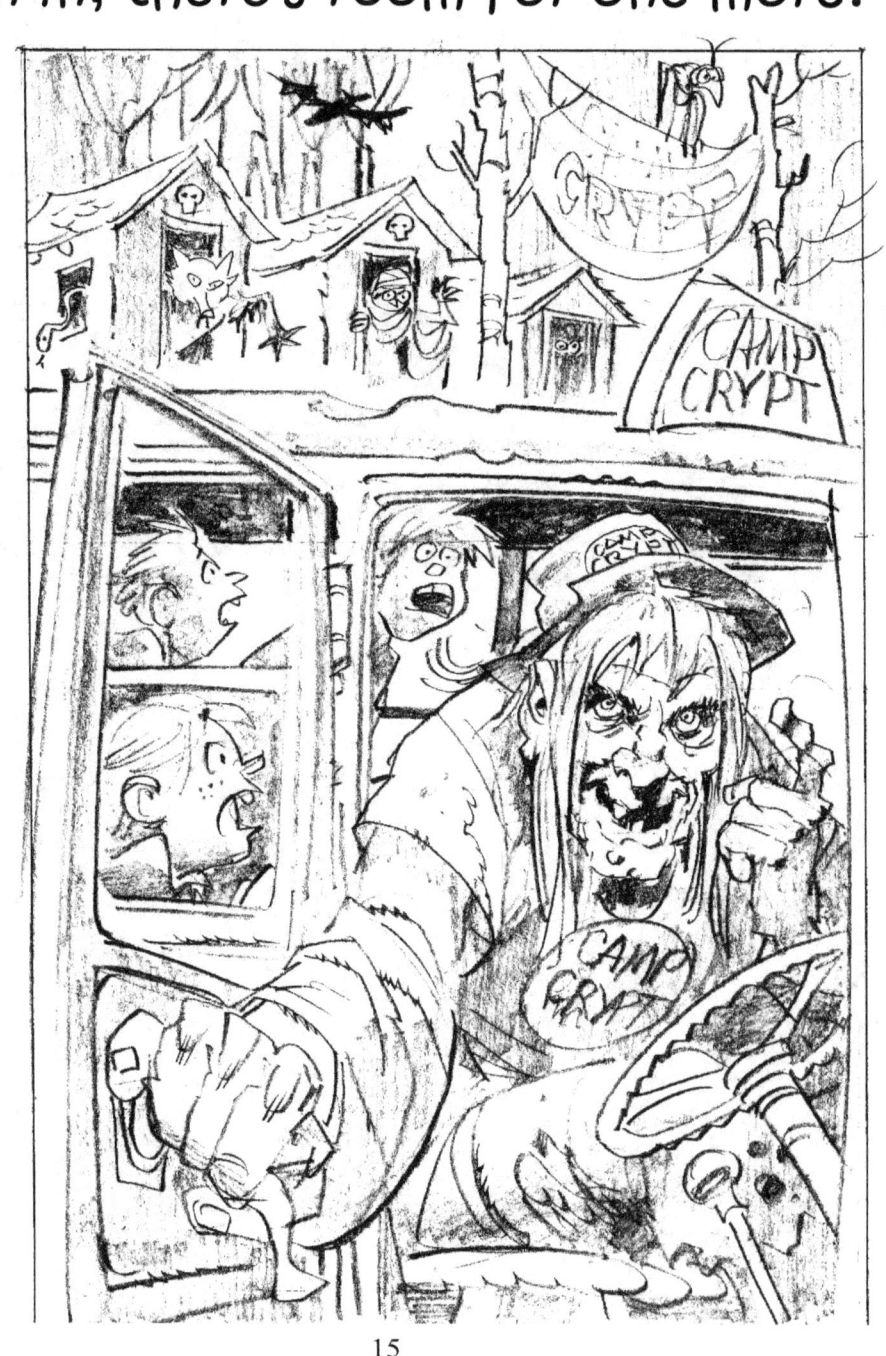

Now for a collection of sketches showing How-to draw a monster... Six easy steps with steps one through four sketching progressively more details in pencil, then step five inking and step six shading. What happen to the monster next is your story?

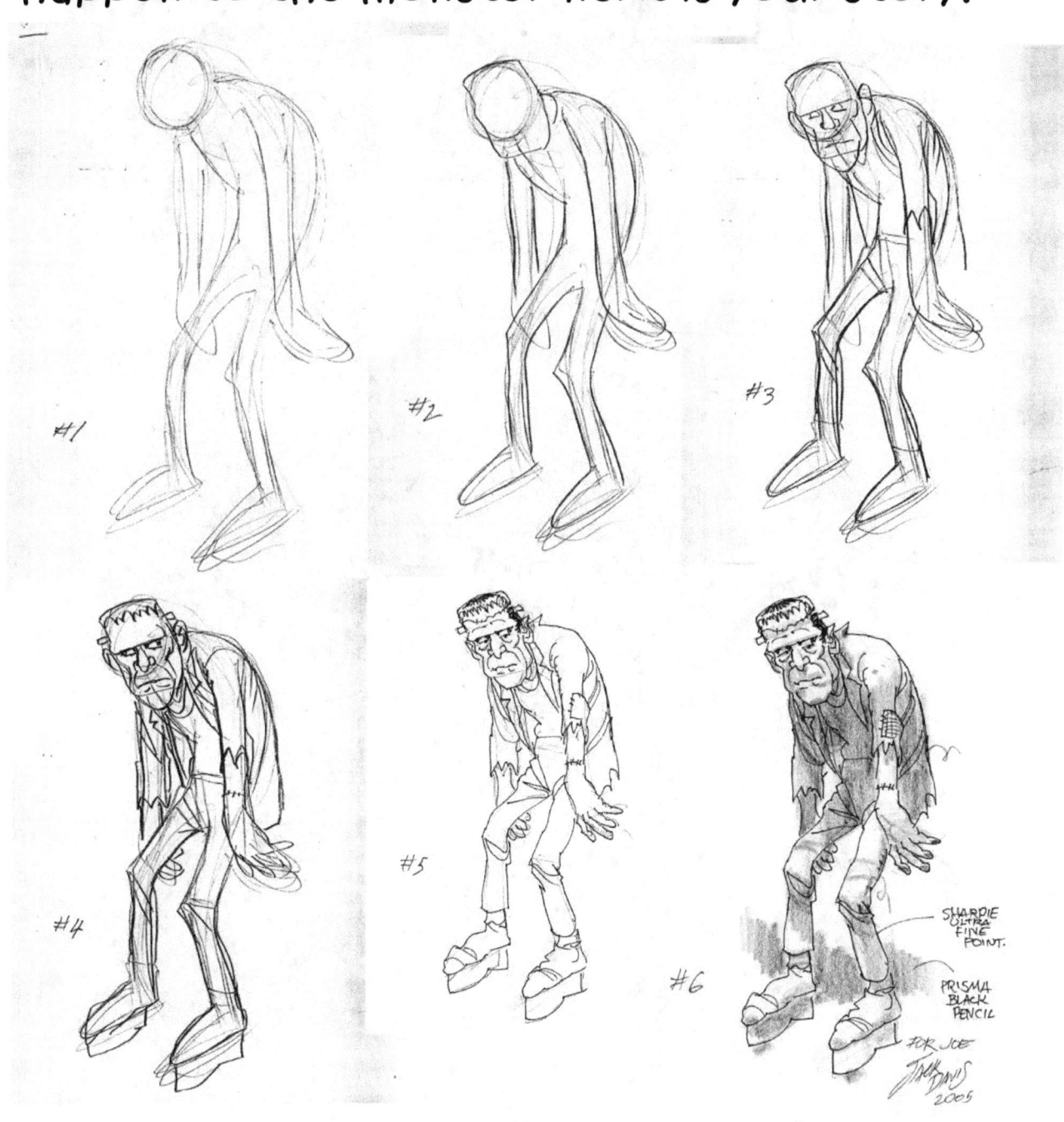

This is a sketch picturing a first aid class showing how to wrap your own Mummy, complete with incantations and curses. Maybe a Mummy will follow you home.

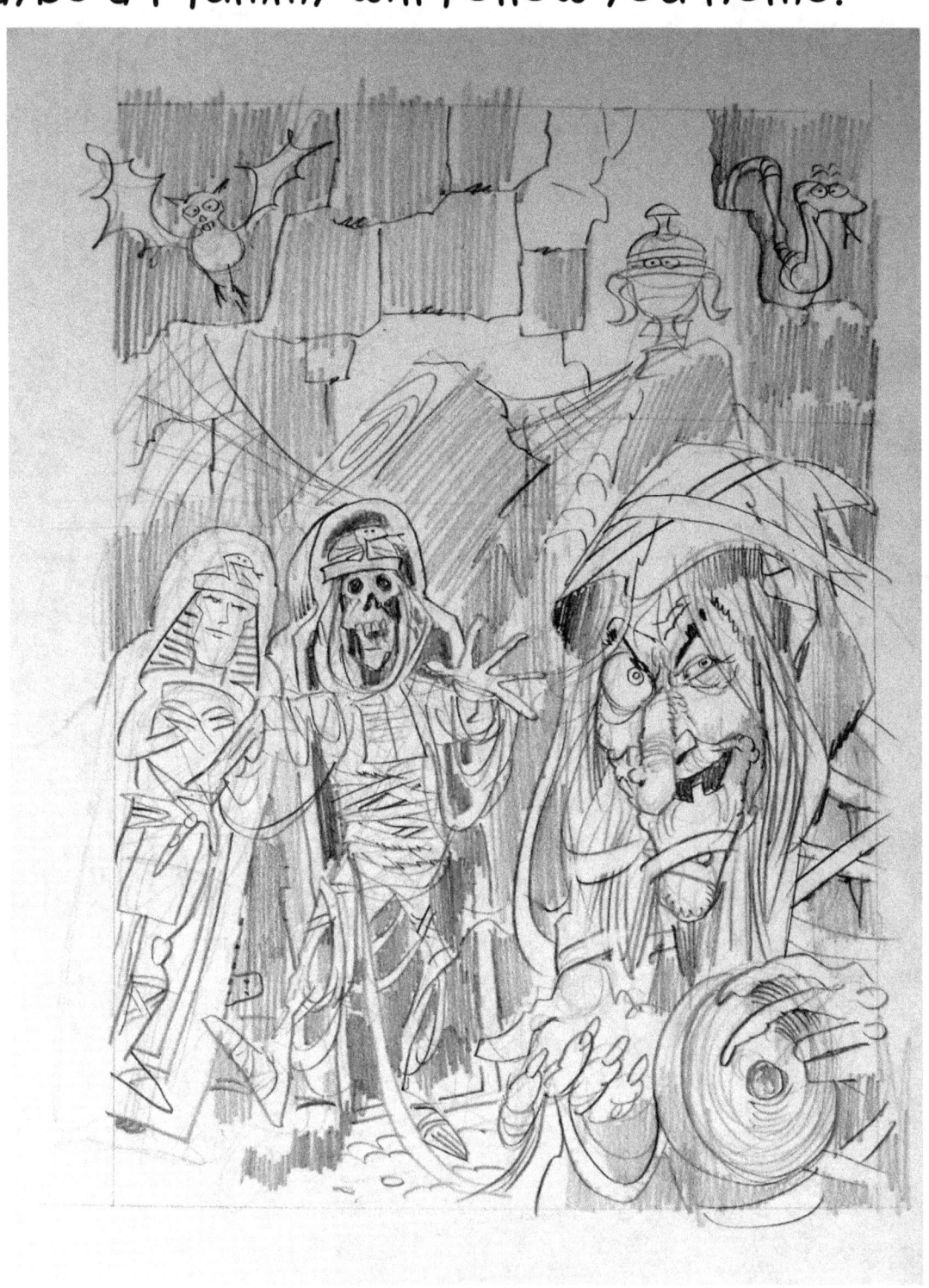

Our next sketch pictures an old Crypt Keeper who had an obsession for digging up the past, but not a past you would want to revisit.

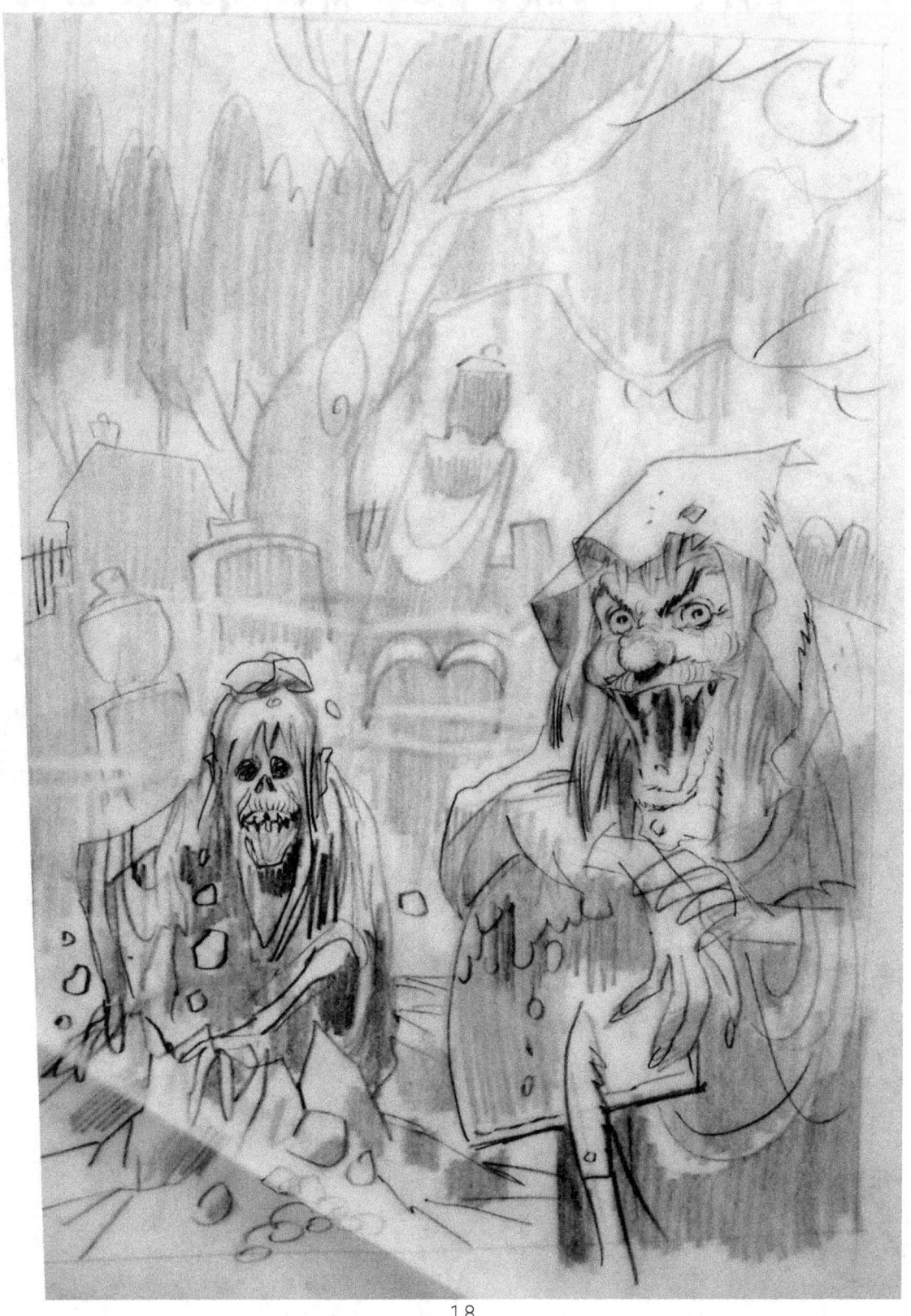

How about this sketch of a class of grade school kids that went on a field trip to a casket making company, but saw much more than they expected?

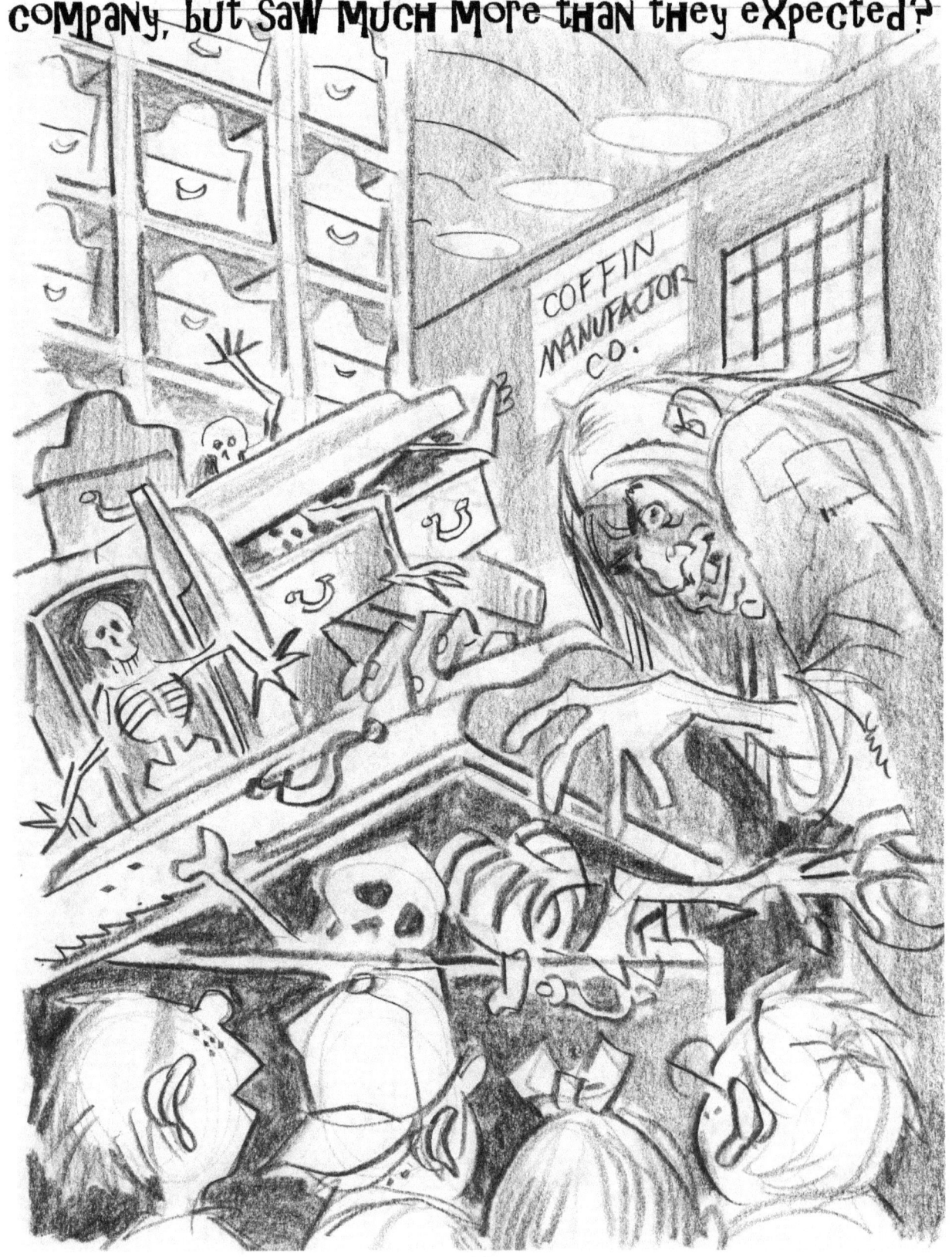

Our next sketch is of a game show that is staged on location at a local cemetery. It looks like the big surprise behind door #3.

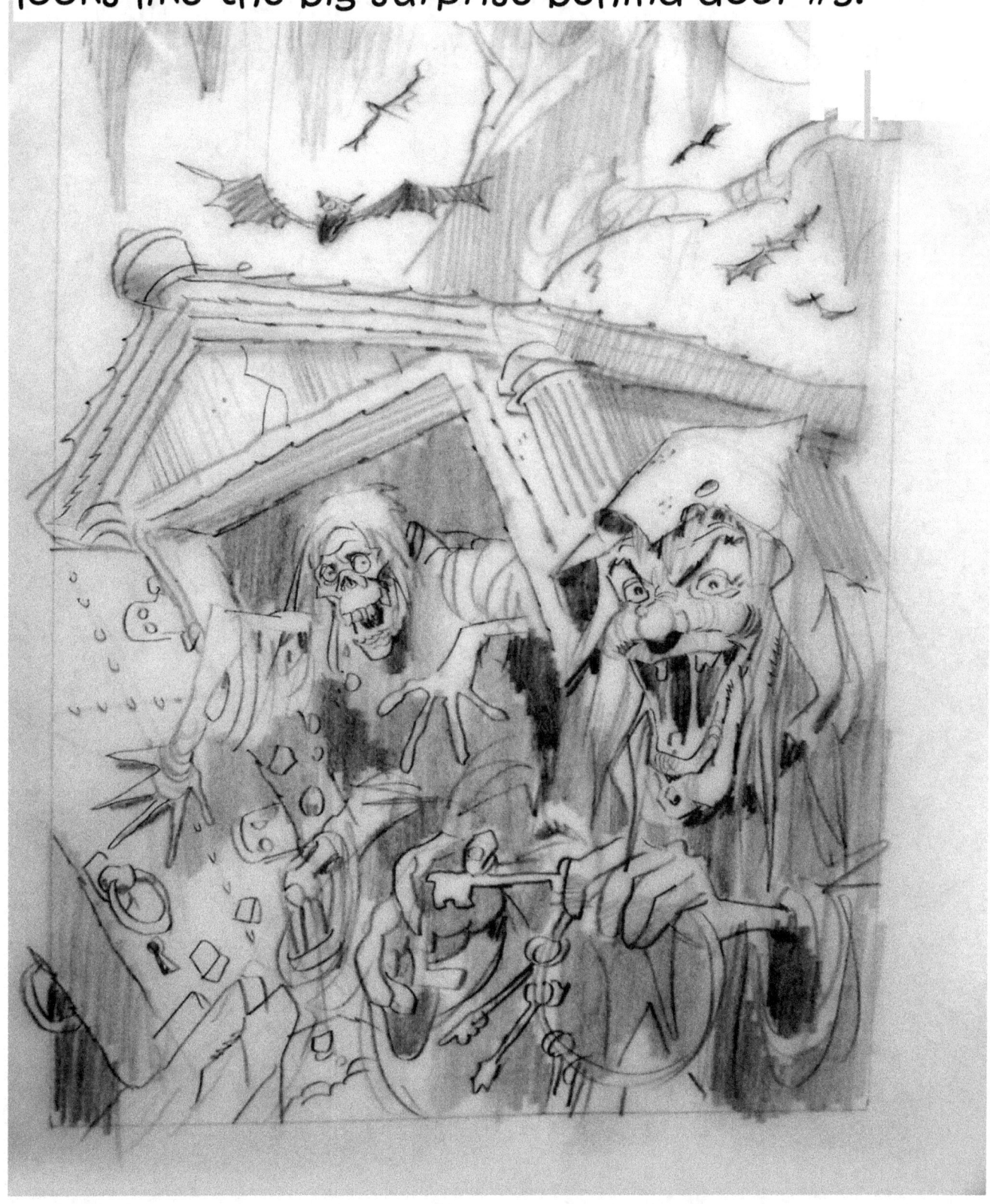

This is a sketch of a simple scientist who was trying to conjure up something he could use to help with the chores around the castle. Unfortunately, it runs on 3,487 D batteries.

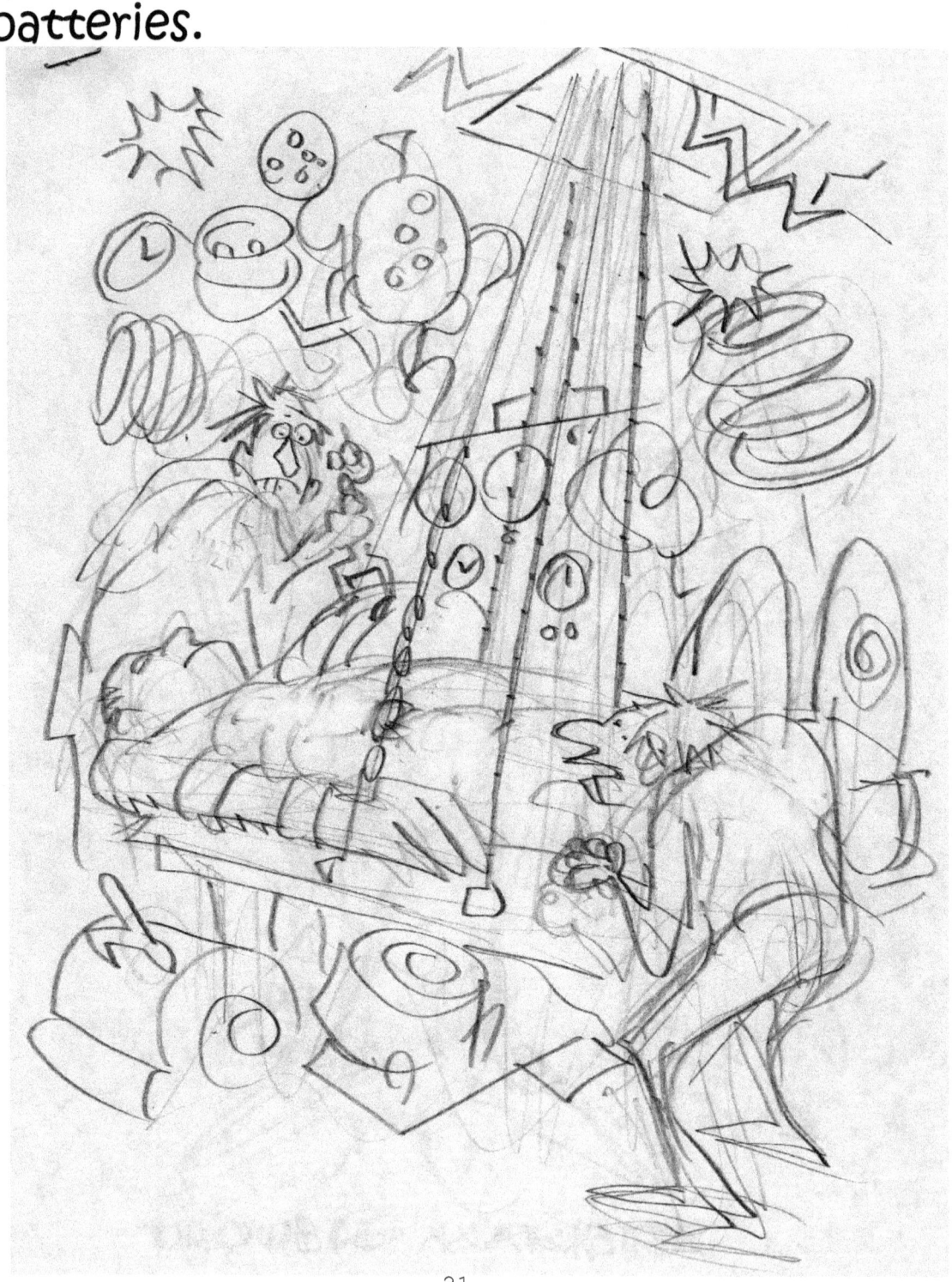

Here's A strange sketch showing a couple of sneaky boys staying up too late one night to watch an Old horror movie about a haunted house, only to be sucked into the movie after falling asleep.

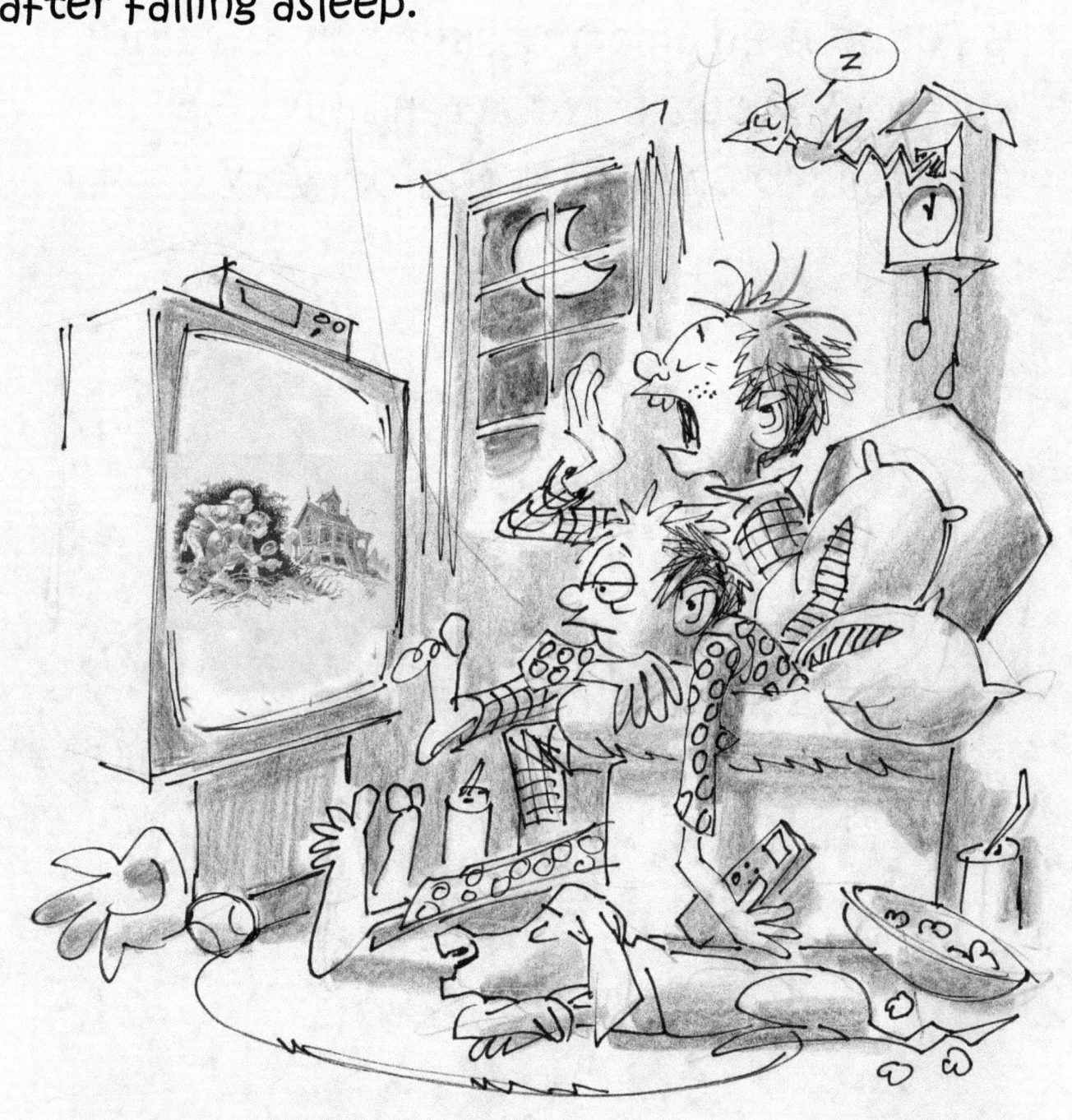

Now for a sketch picturing a careless hearse driver who loses a casket as he speeds over a bump in the road. Upon returning to collect the lost cargo all that is found is an empty casket...that is until the body shows up to attend his own funeral. No charge on this delivery.

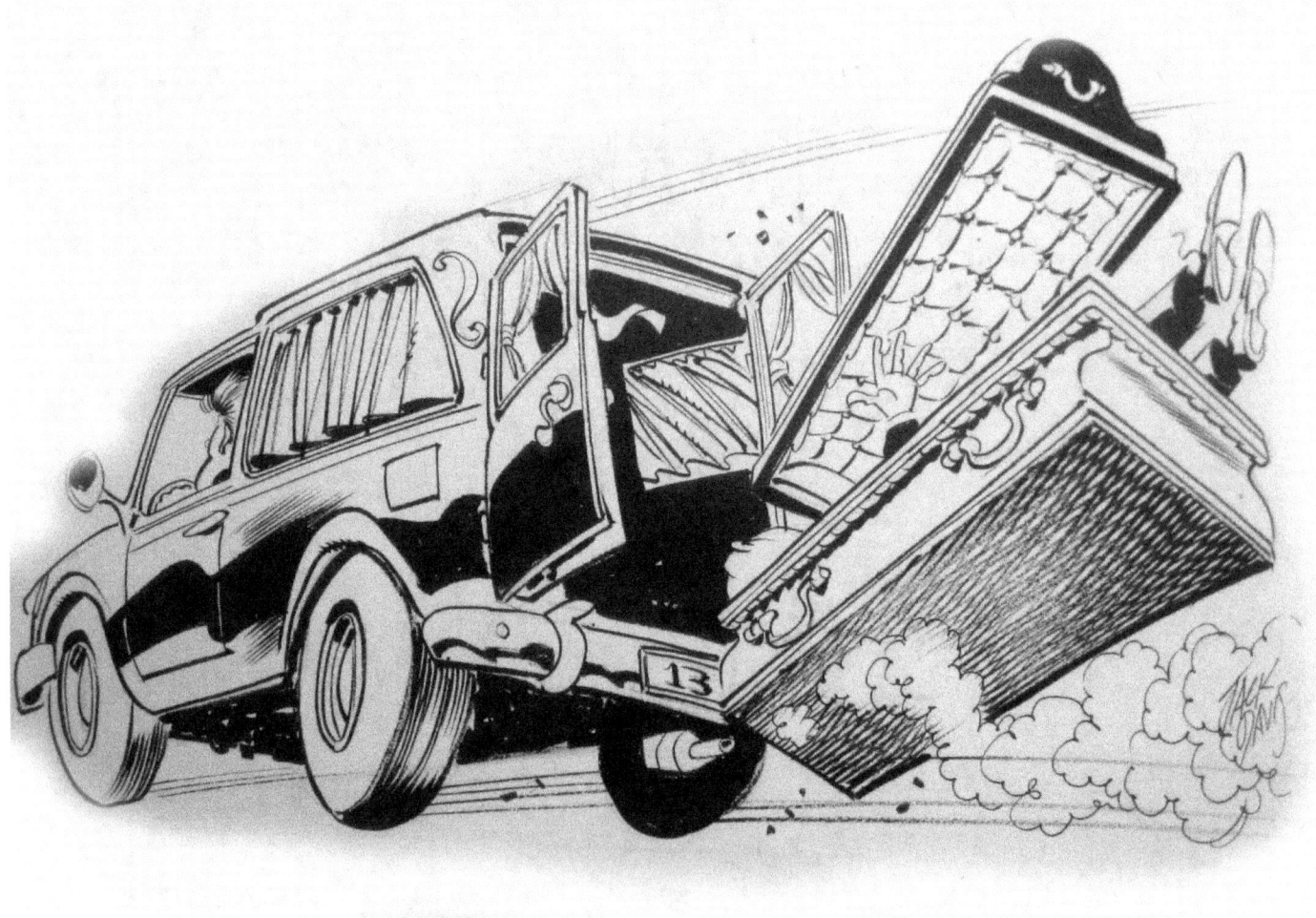

Our next sketch displays a Mad Shoemaker who enchants each pair of shoes to cause the wearer to gradually fade away... and return as a ghost of their former self. Great way to lose weight.

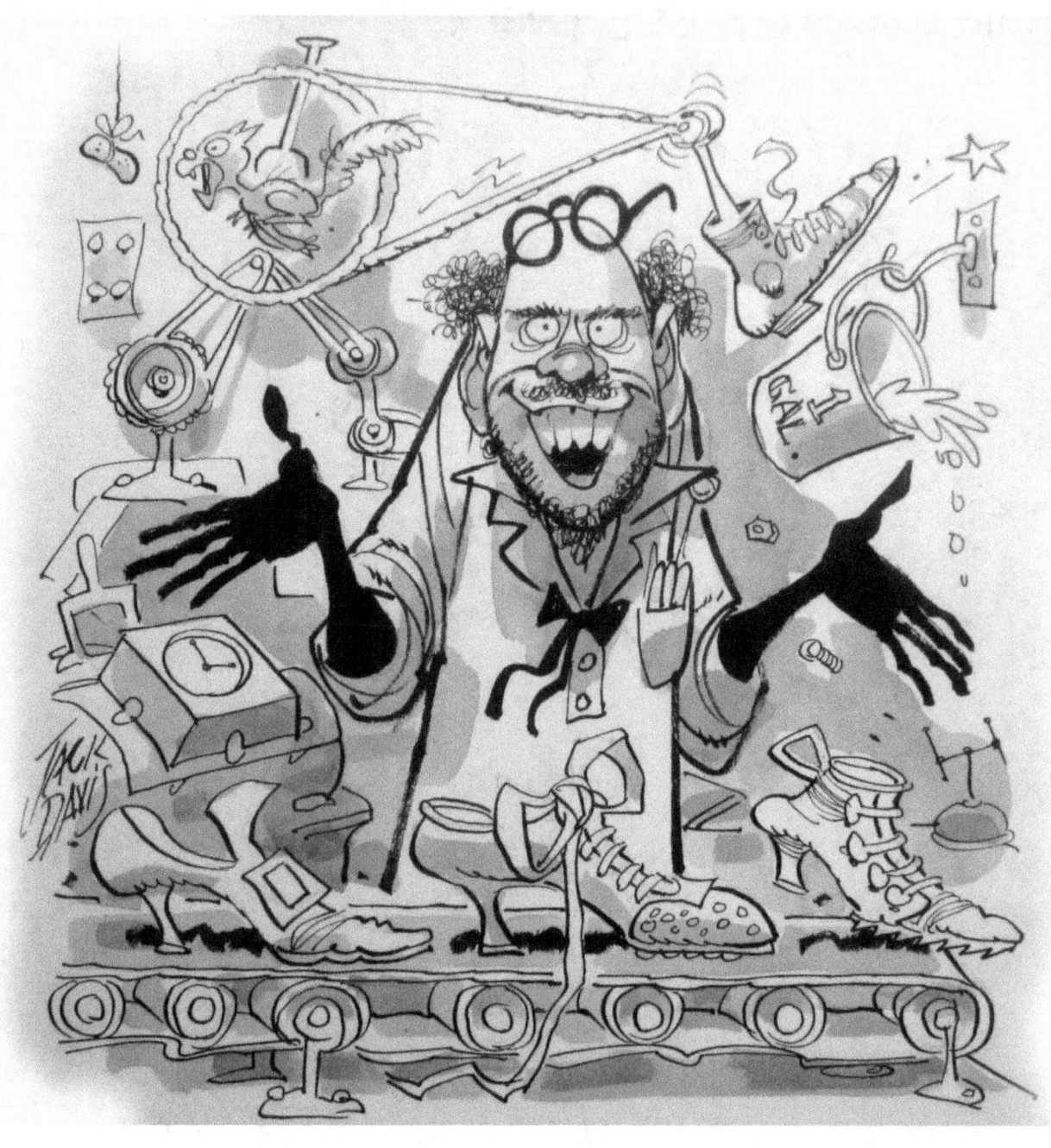

This sketch is a bit unusual, most bugs seldom show fear, but when they enter a haunted house and encounter a ghost with a fly swatter it paints a whole new story. Even the landlord got to meet him by surprise. Time to call Ghost Busters!

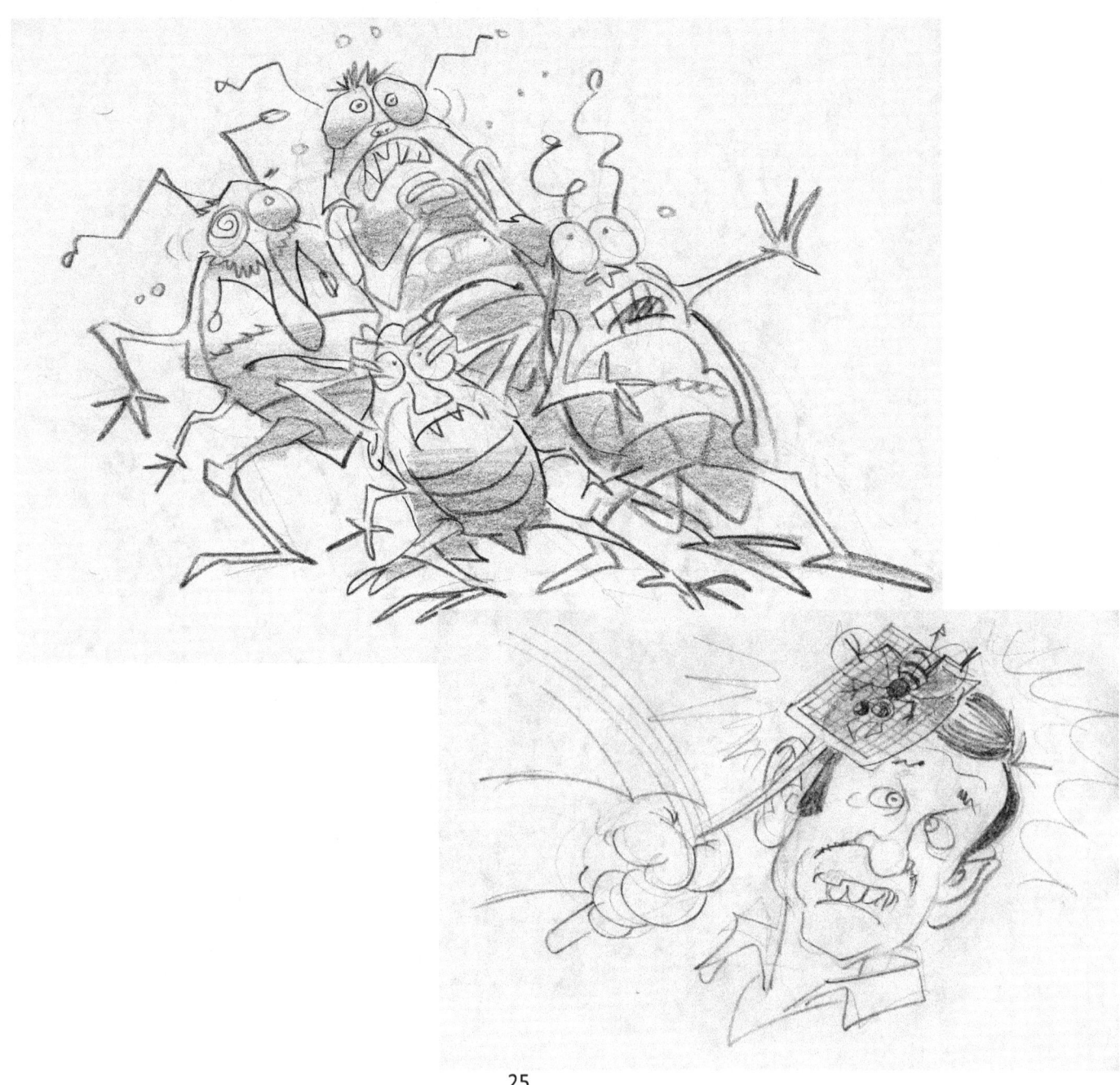

Now for an amusing sketch of a happy family celebrating the Halloween holiday with a pizza party. Unfortunately for them the pizza box that mysteriously showed up on their door step that evening was hungrier than they were. All that was found the next day were the family's costumes and hats.

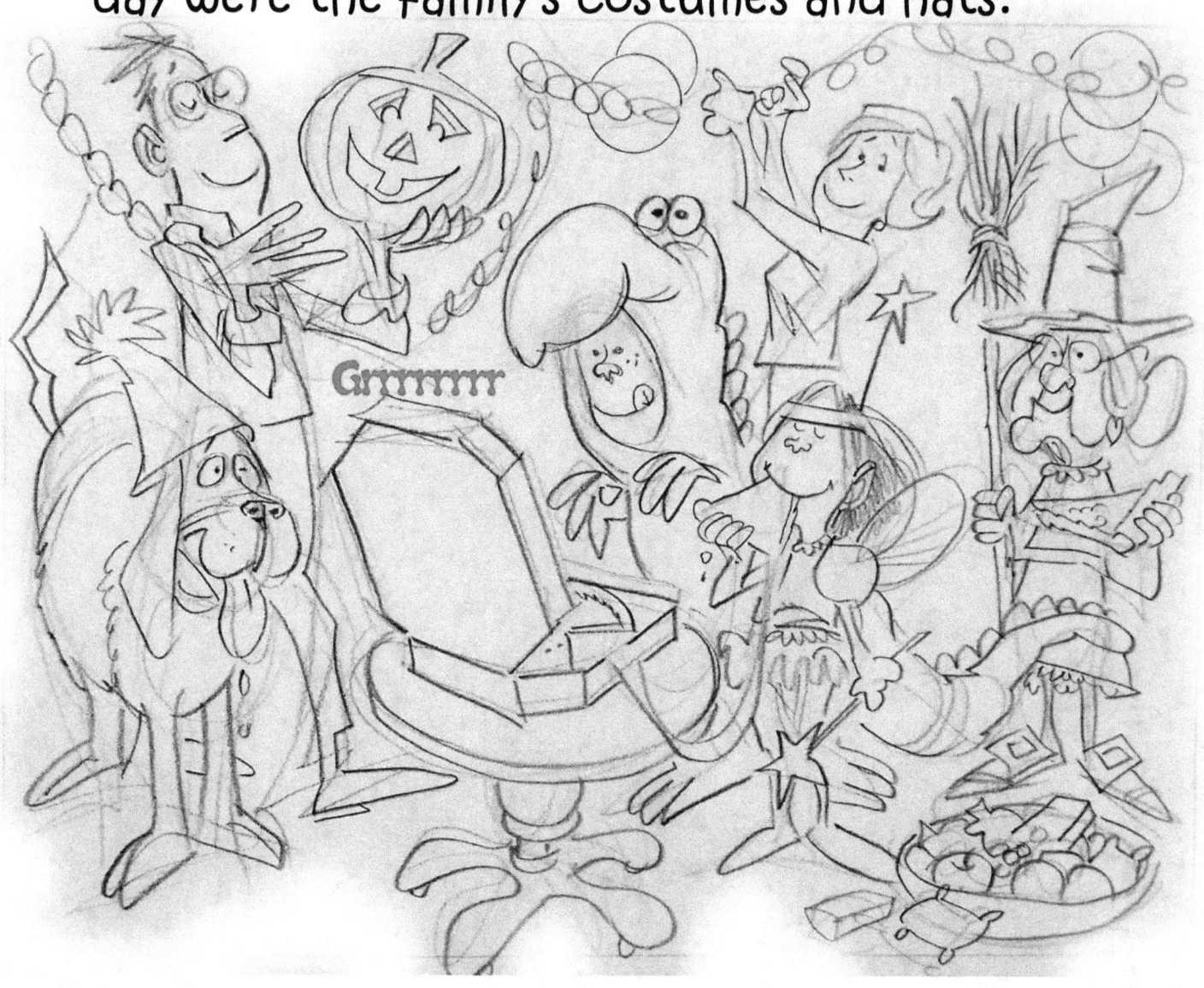

This was a group sketch of what some hikers saw who came across a large campfire in the remote spot of a dense forest. While hiding, they watched what appeared to be a father-son monster party being conducted around a huge campfire under a full moon. A disturbing new twist to scouting.

Our next sketch is about a couple of curios boys who decided to take a dare and climb up some rickety old stairs to the haunted attic of their foster house, getting out alive wasn't nearly as easy.

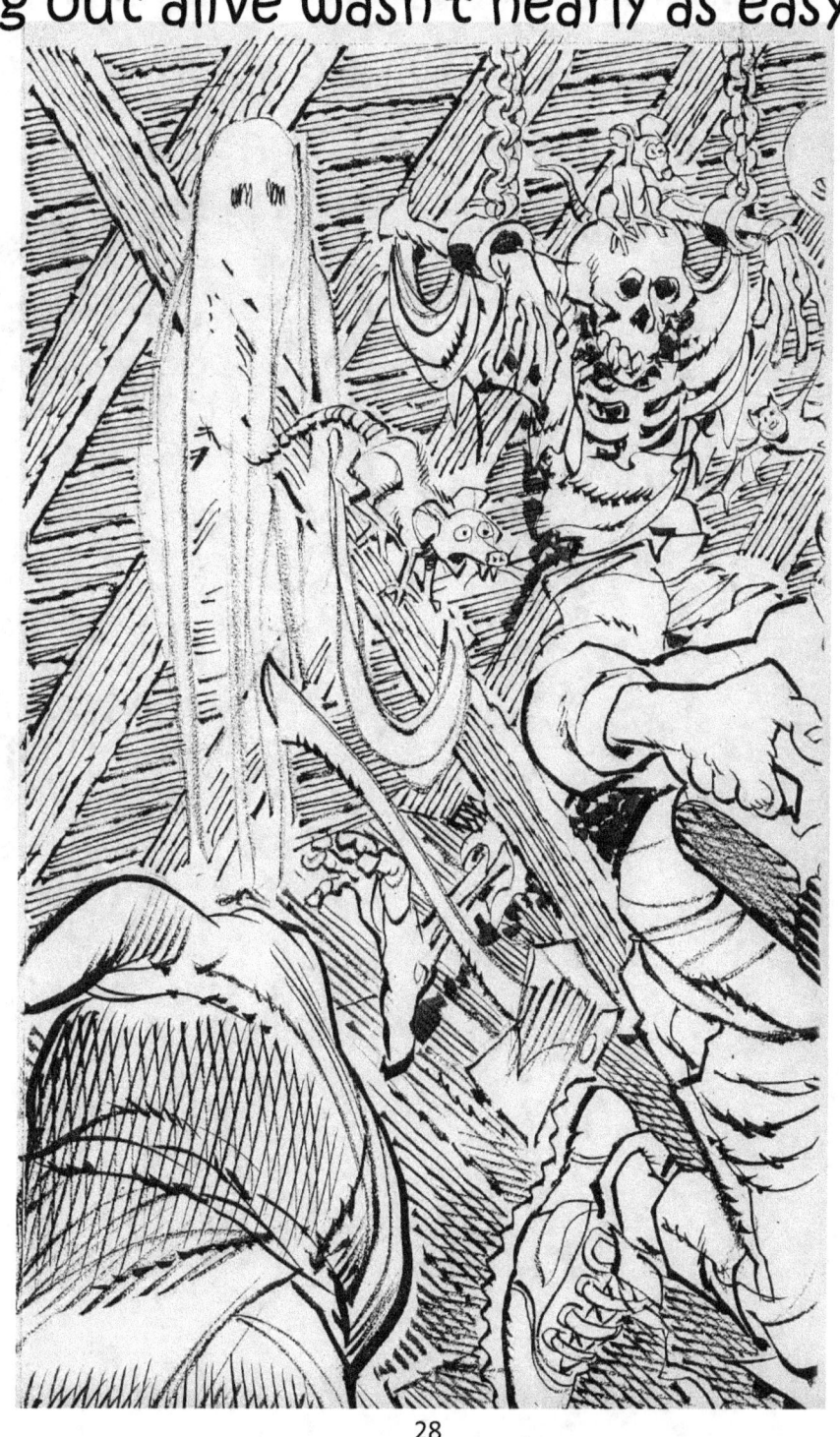

This spooky sketch is of a enchanted wooded area where hunters and hikers would mysteriously go missing. Now we can see why. The unsuspecting hiker in this sketch came across an unusual glowing worm, but when he held it up for a closer look he soon discovered it was just bait for a trap set by the lightening witch.

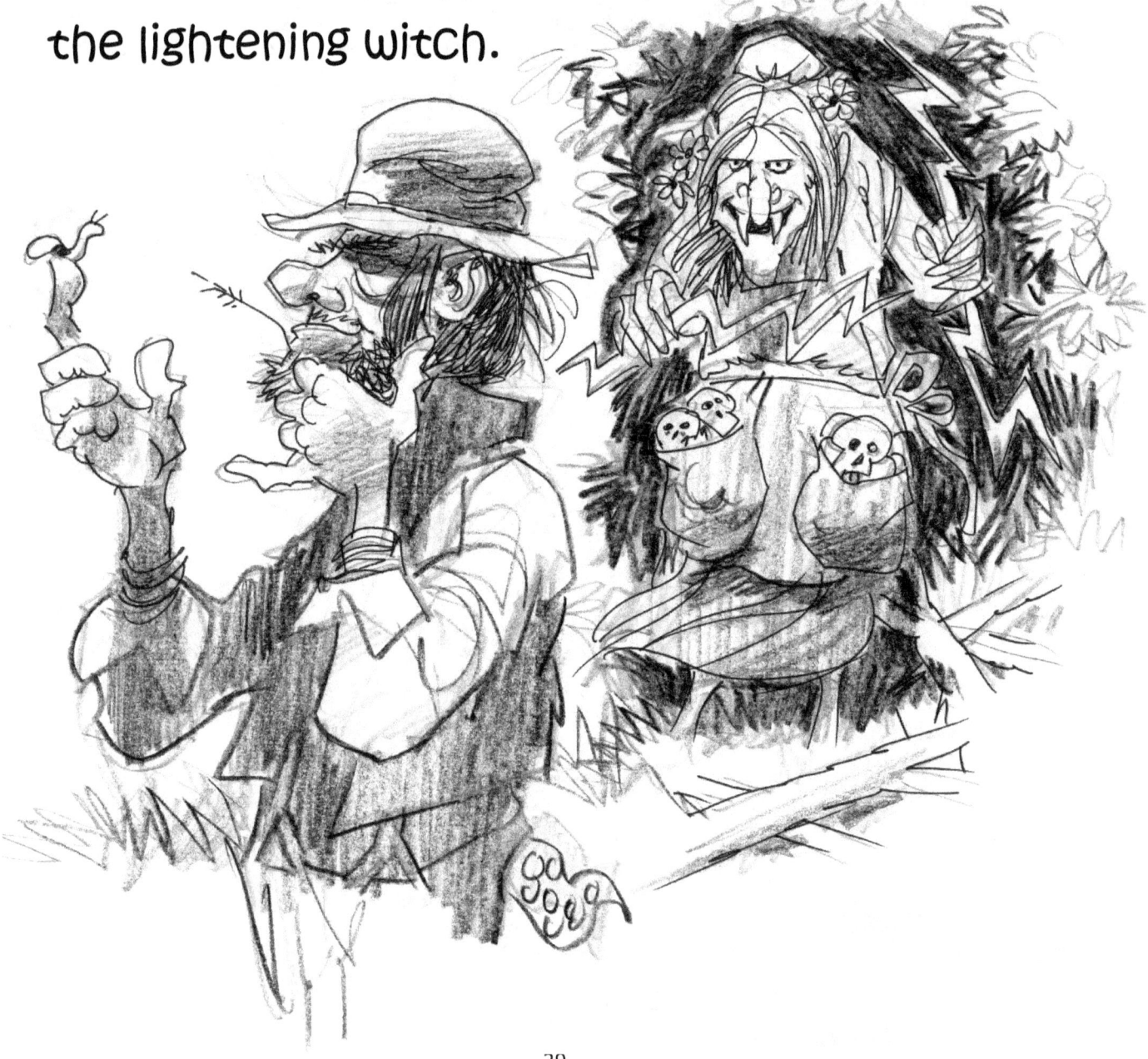

Now for a mystery sketch about a swampy area where local fishermen were complaining about something scaring away all the fish. After noticing an extremely strong fish stench this fisherman unfortunately discovered the source of the fish disappearances.

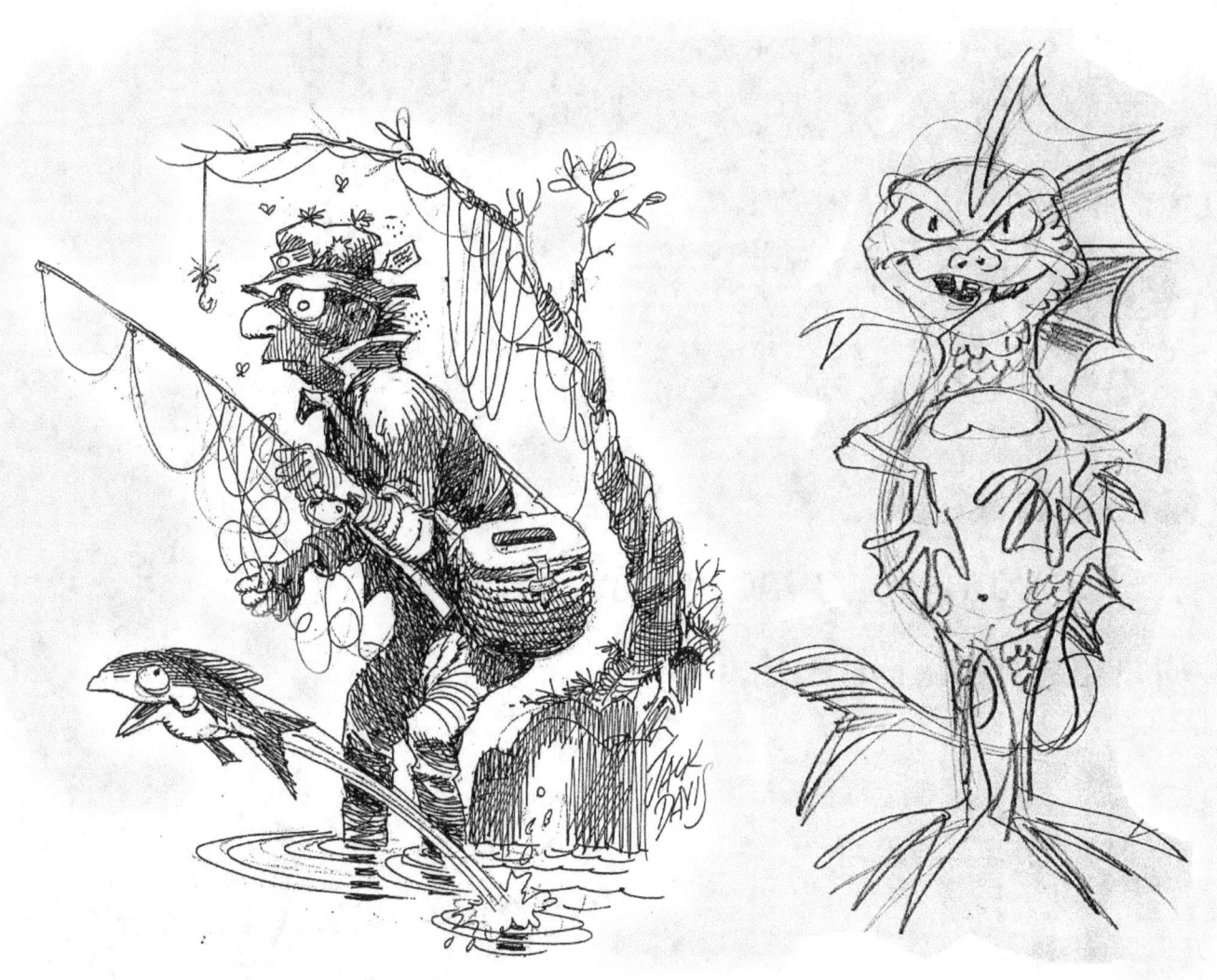

This next sketch shows a rodeo clown who made the mistake of jumping into a haunted barrel. When he popped his head back out, he realized that he wasn't in Kansas anymore.

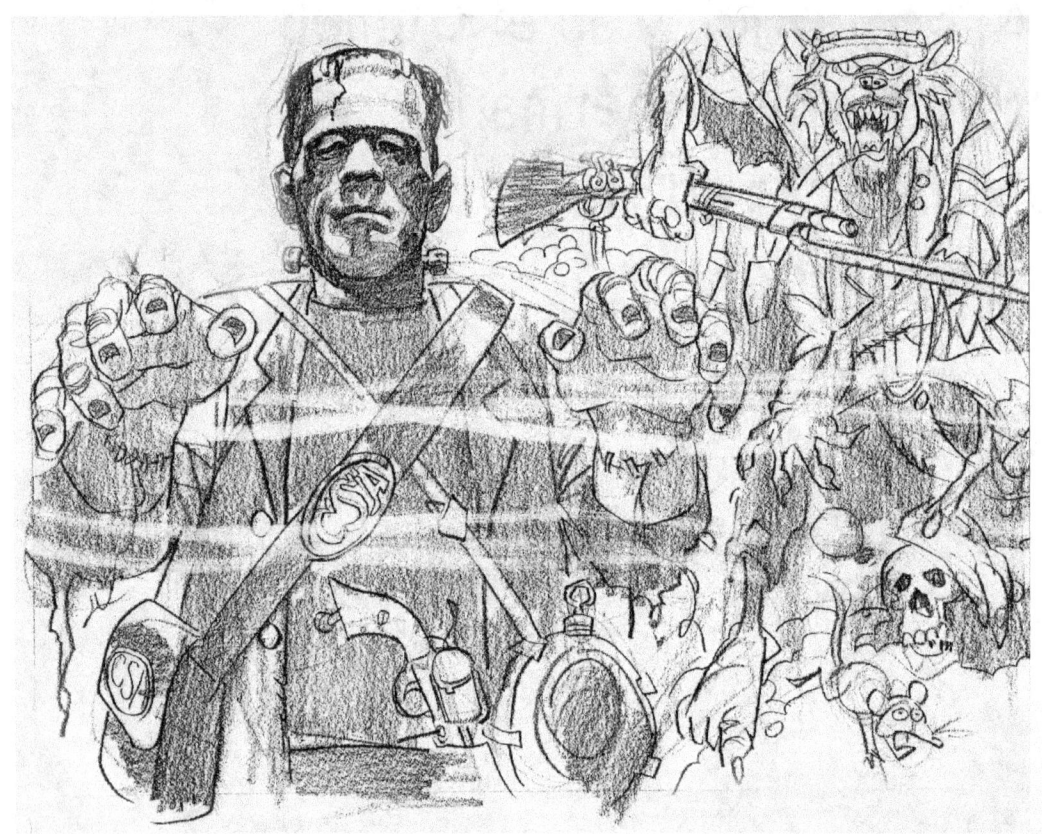

... Just what do monsters do with clowns anyway?

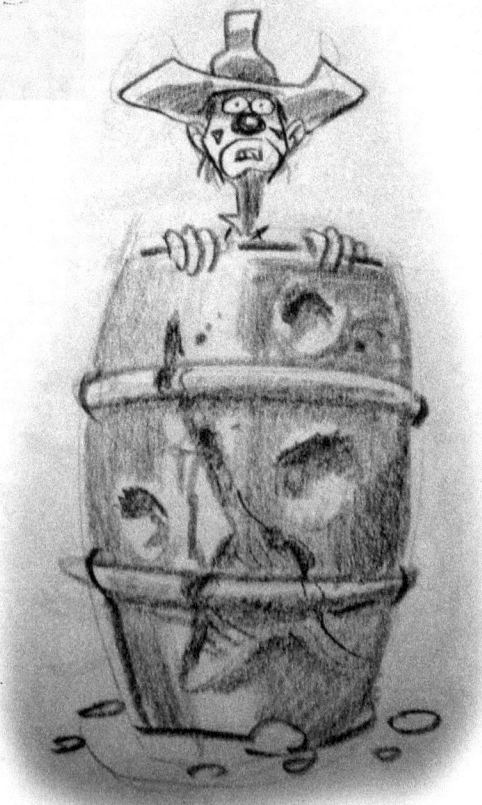

Our next sketch pictures a strange midnight gathering of the most unexpected bed fellows who converged over an old bridge to enjoy and share a collection of horror comic books they discovered that had fallen off a passing Amazon delivery truck.

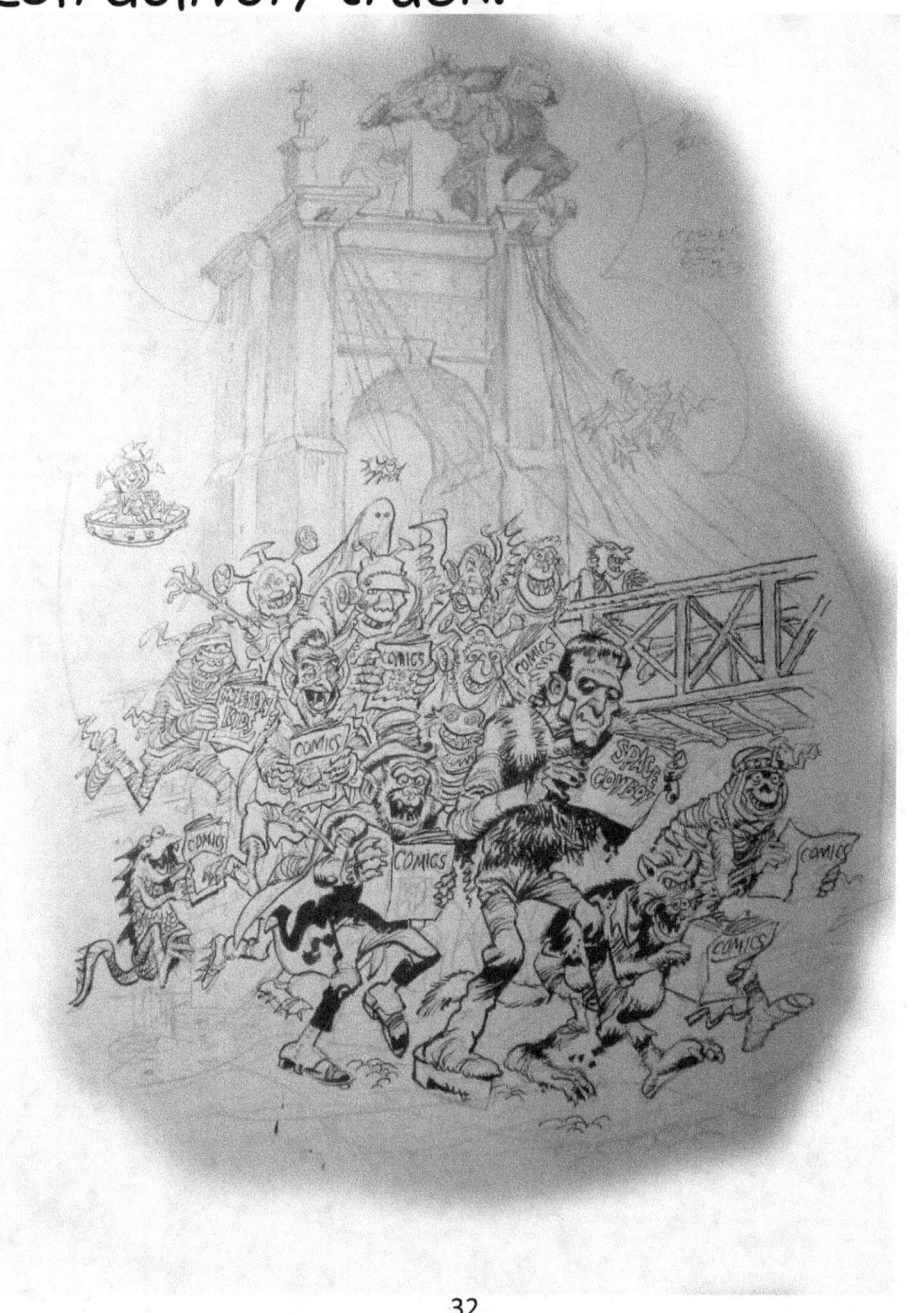

Oh, we forgot to mention, this sketch showing Jack's cleaning lady Victoria, who unfortunately, they had to let go because she would only come out to work between midnight and three am. She was sound asleep in her coffin the rest of the day.

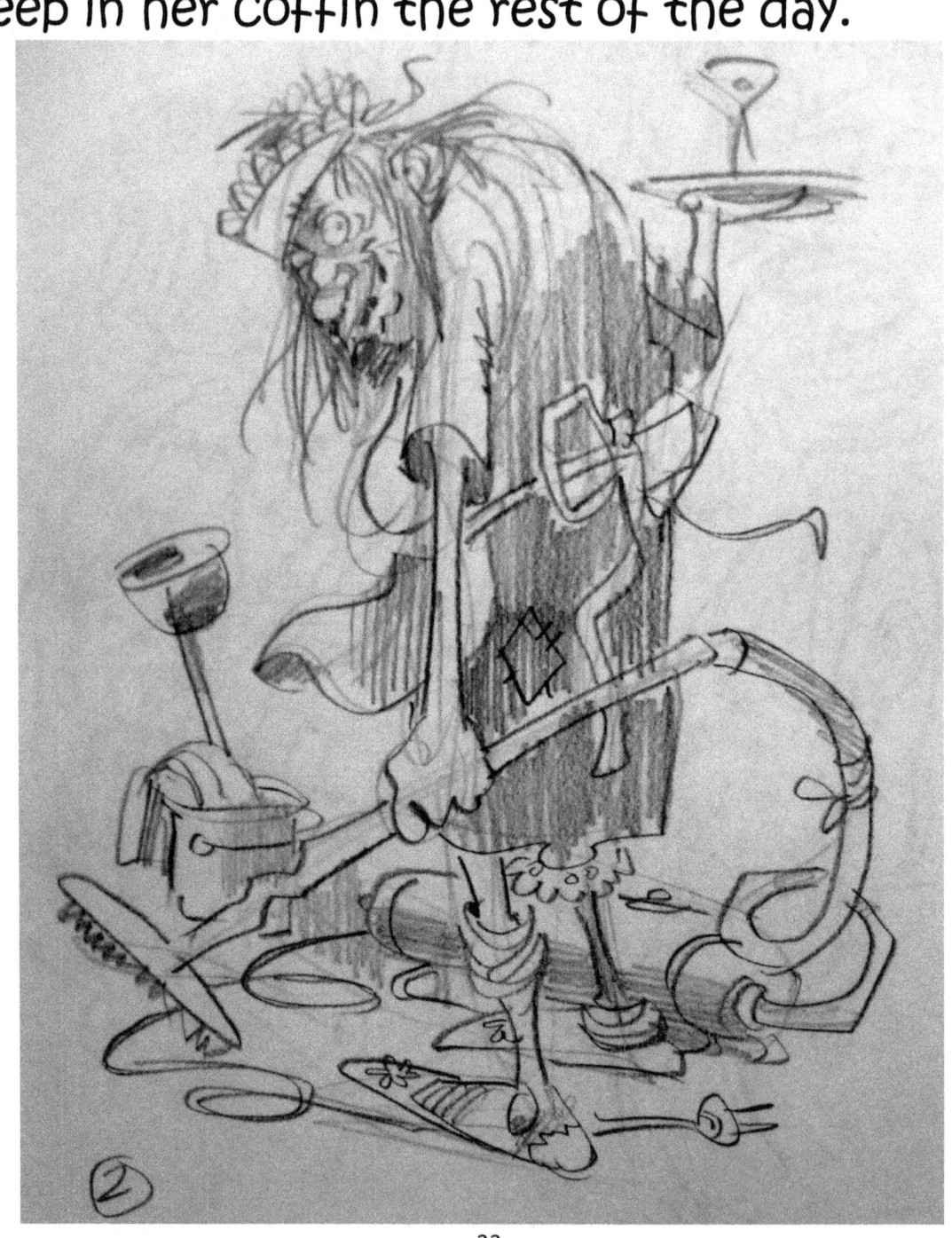

Jonny thought he had found a secret wishing well, but unfortunately, he certainly did not get the wish he asked for.

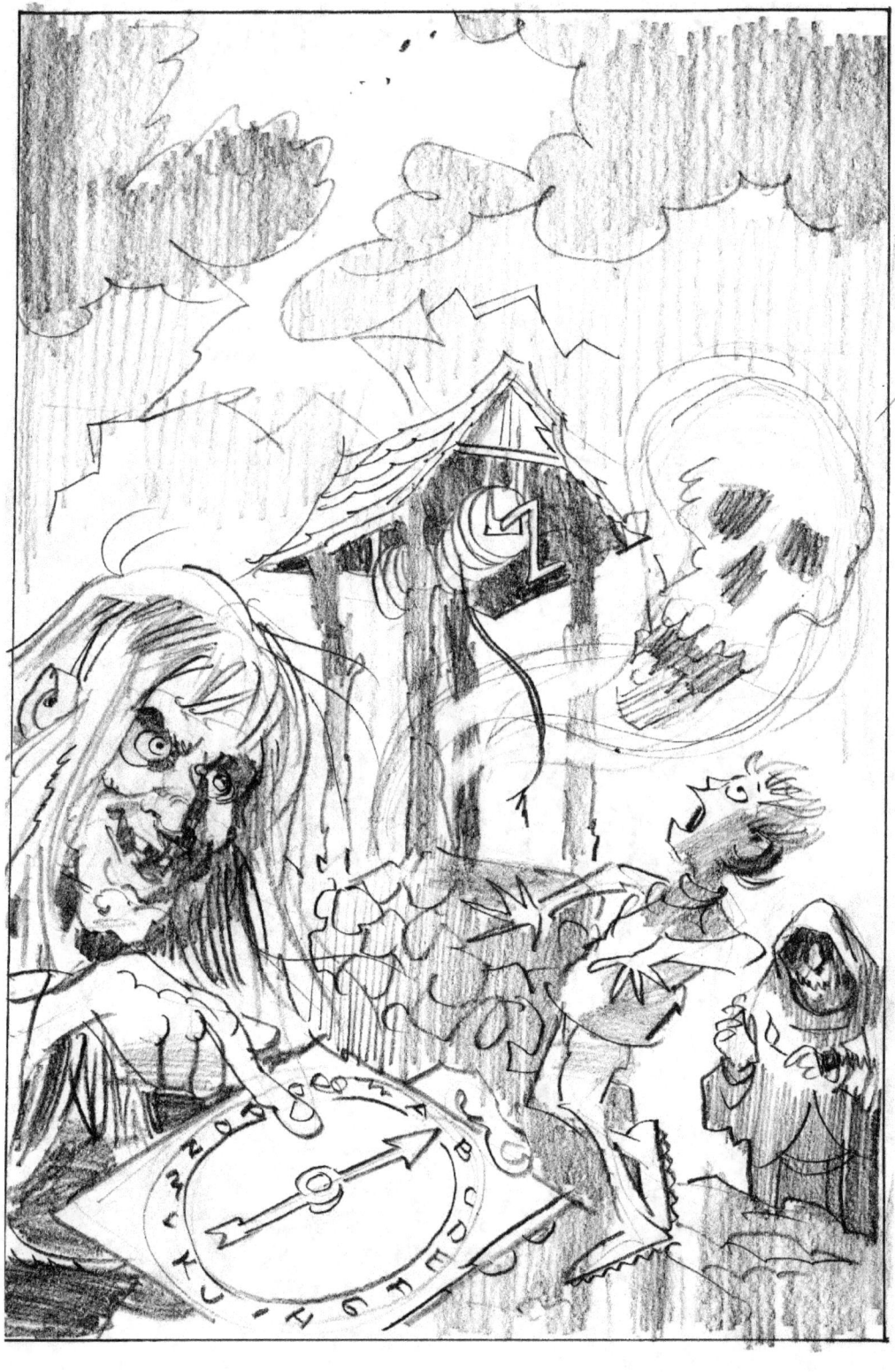

In this sketch we find a group of highly agitated students from Monster U. rushing up to complain about the grade they received in an Advanced Frightology class they took.

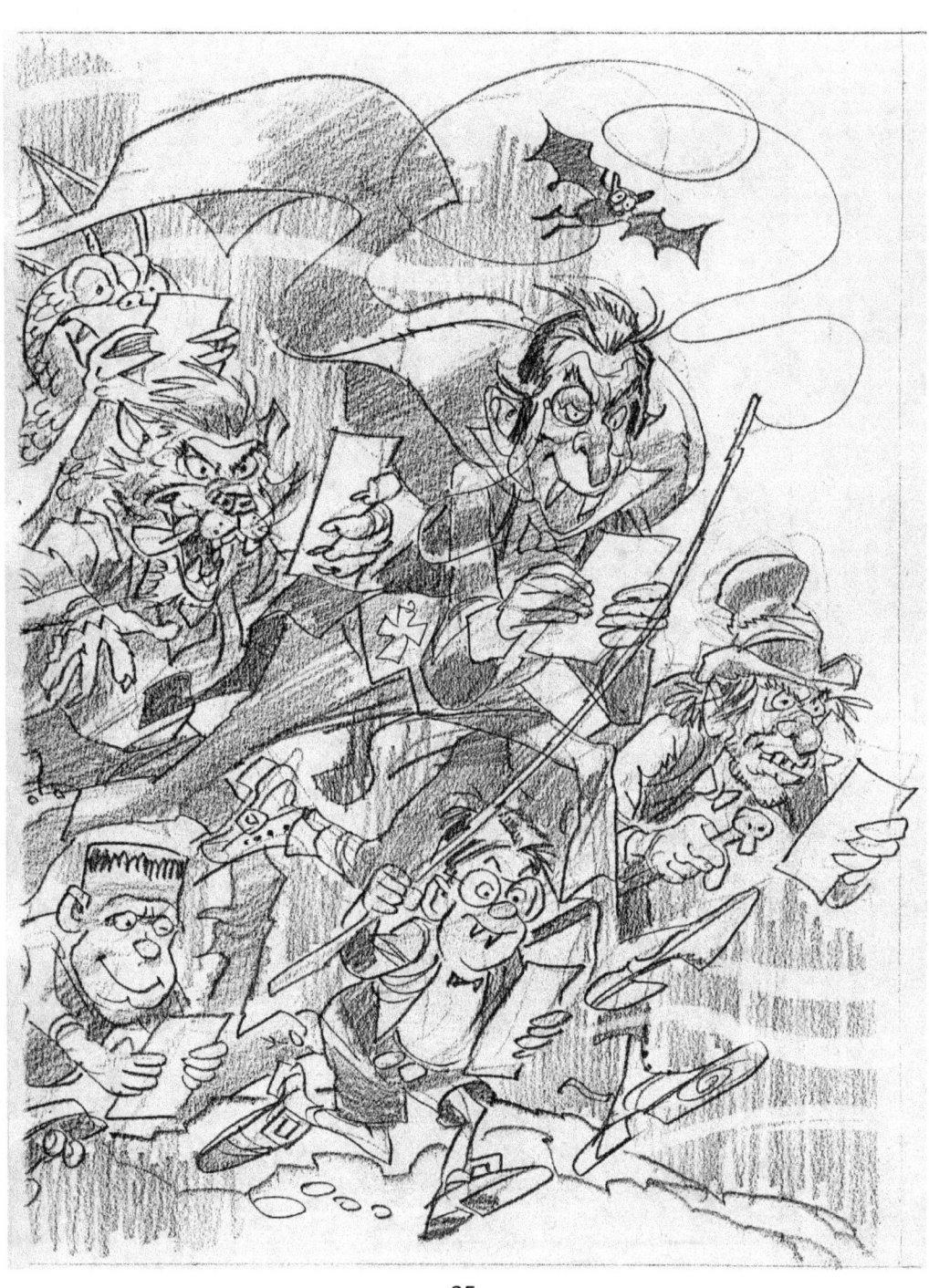

Students from the night class in Frightology also experienced the same disappointment.

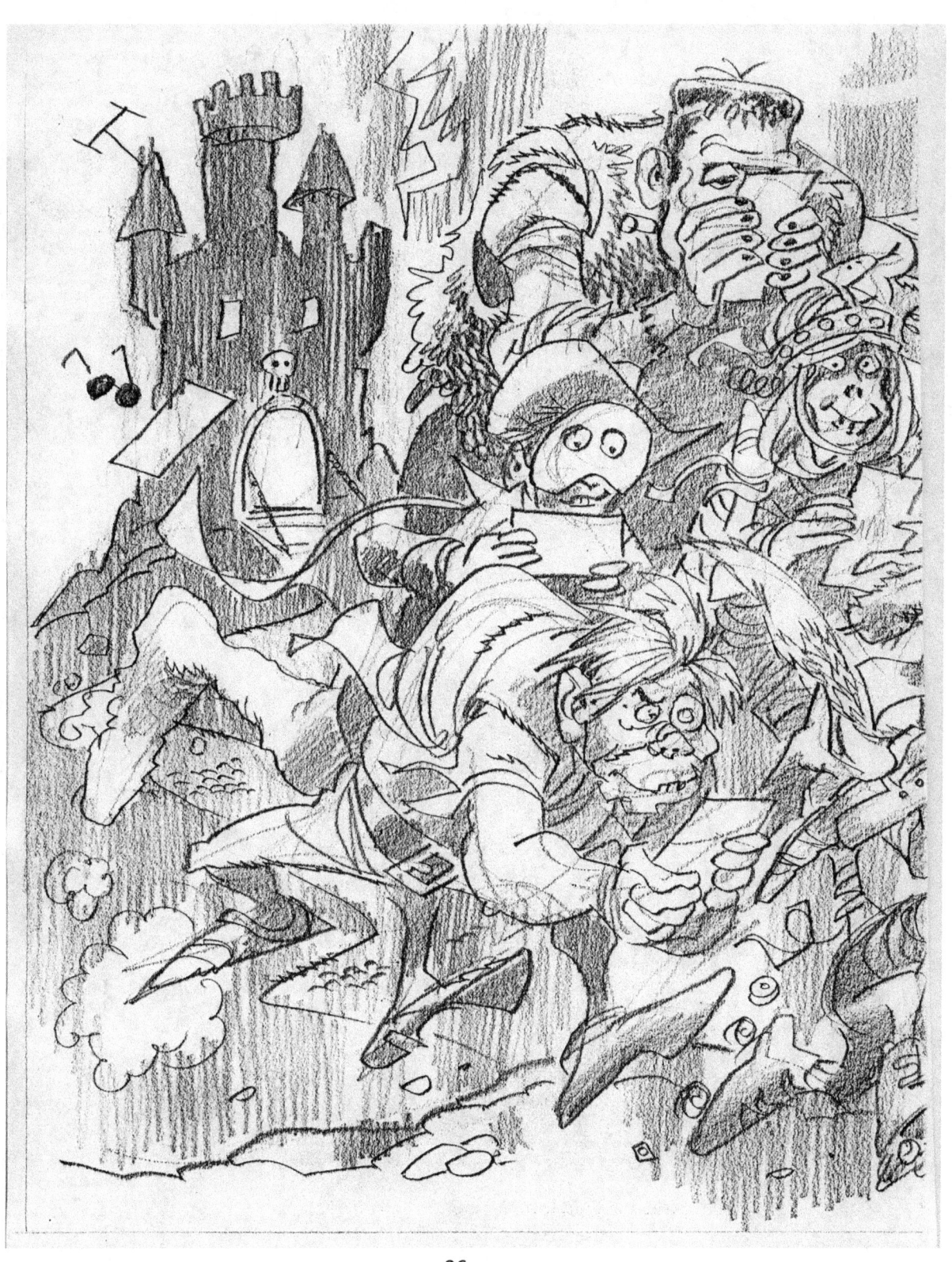

In this sketch we find that not all stories about young Frankenstein were as tragic as the movie.

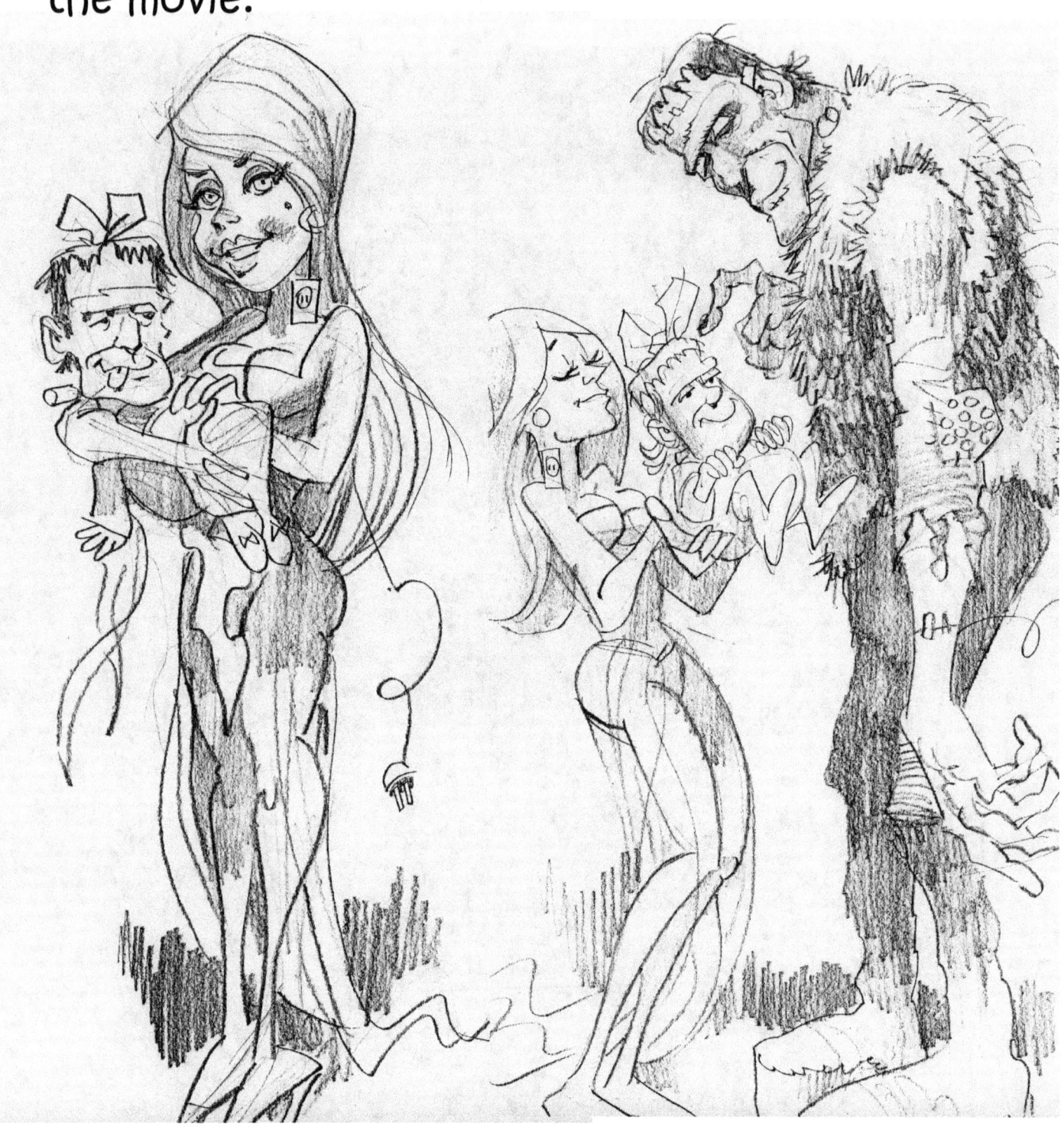

Another sketch shows what happen to an angry little boy who ran away from home and thought the cave he found to live in was uninhabited.

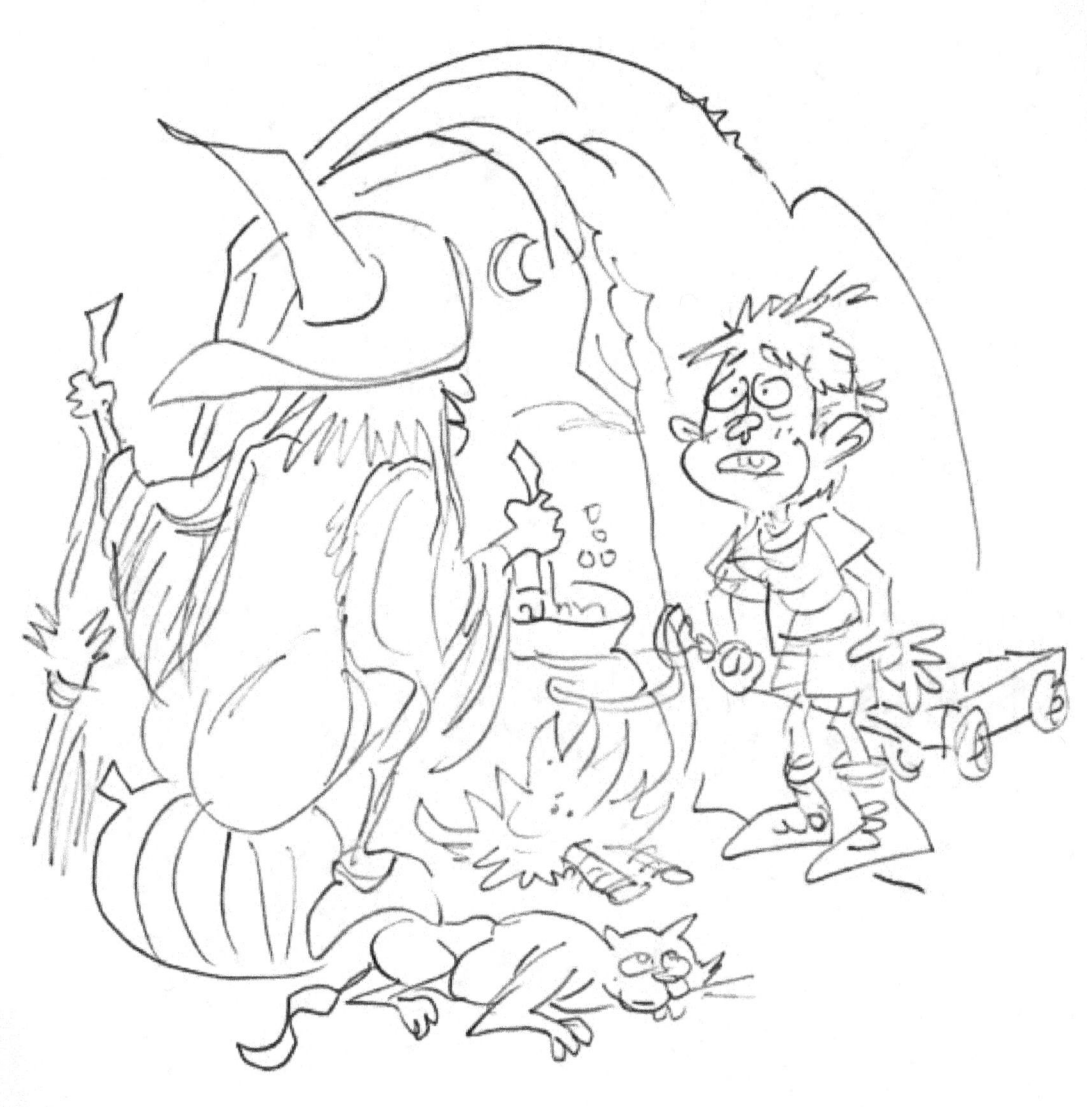

In this sketch the same little boy found the old pumpkin patch by the cemetery was also occupied by a prior howling tenet.

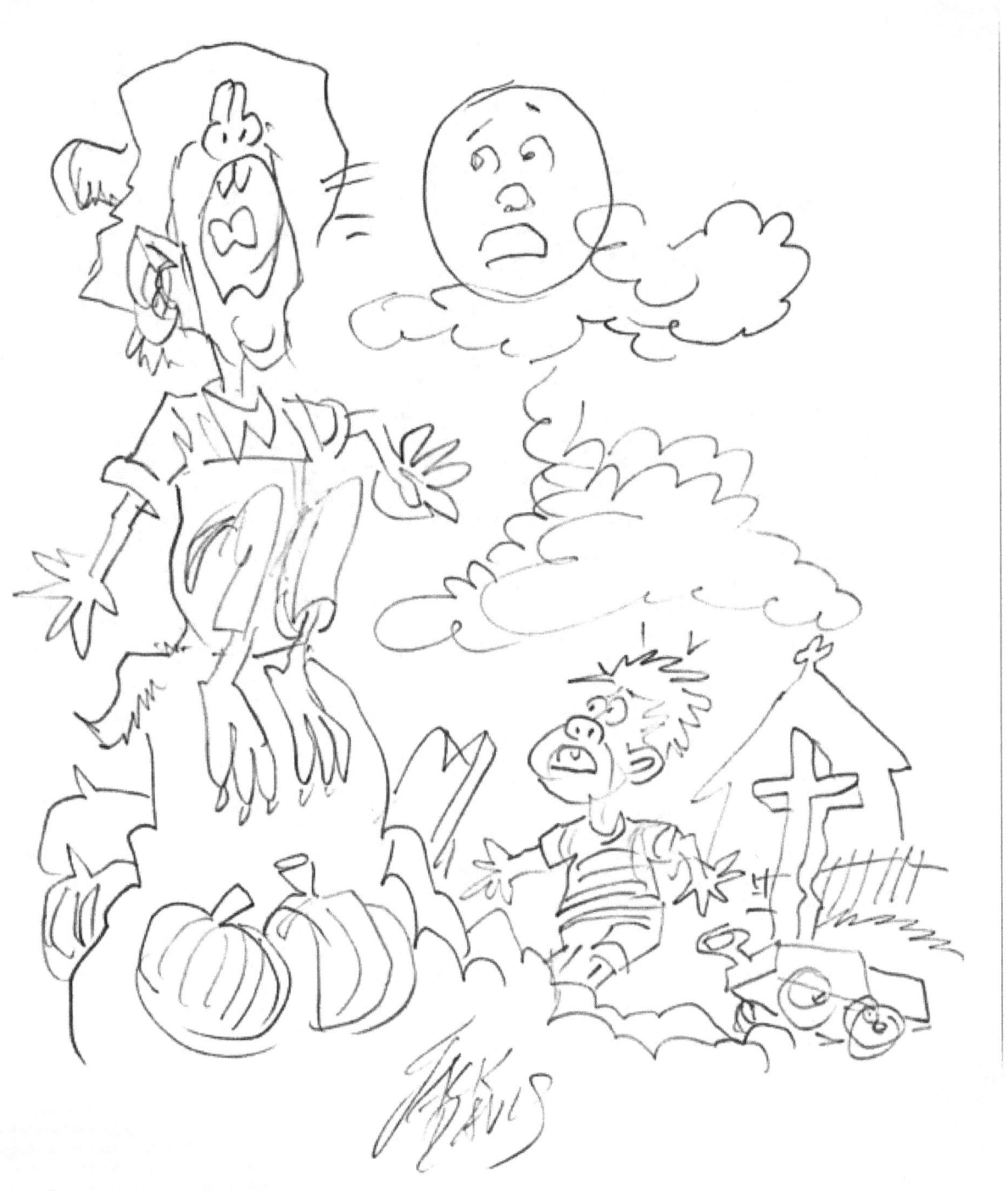

This sketch shows how some of the best smellin pumpkins may contain unwanted guest that are released during the carving.

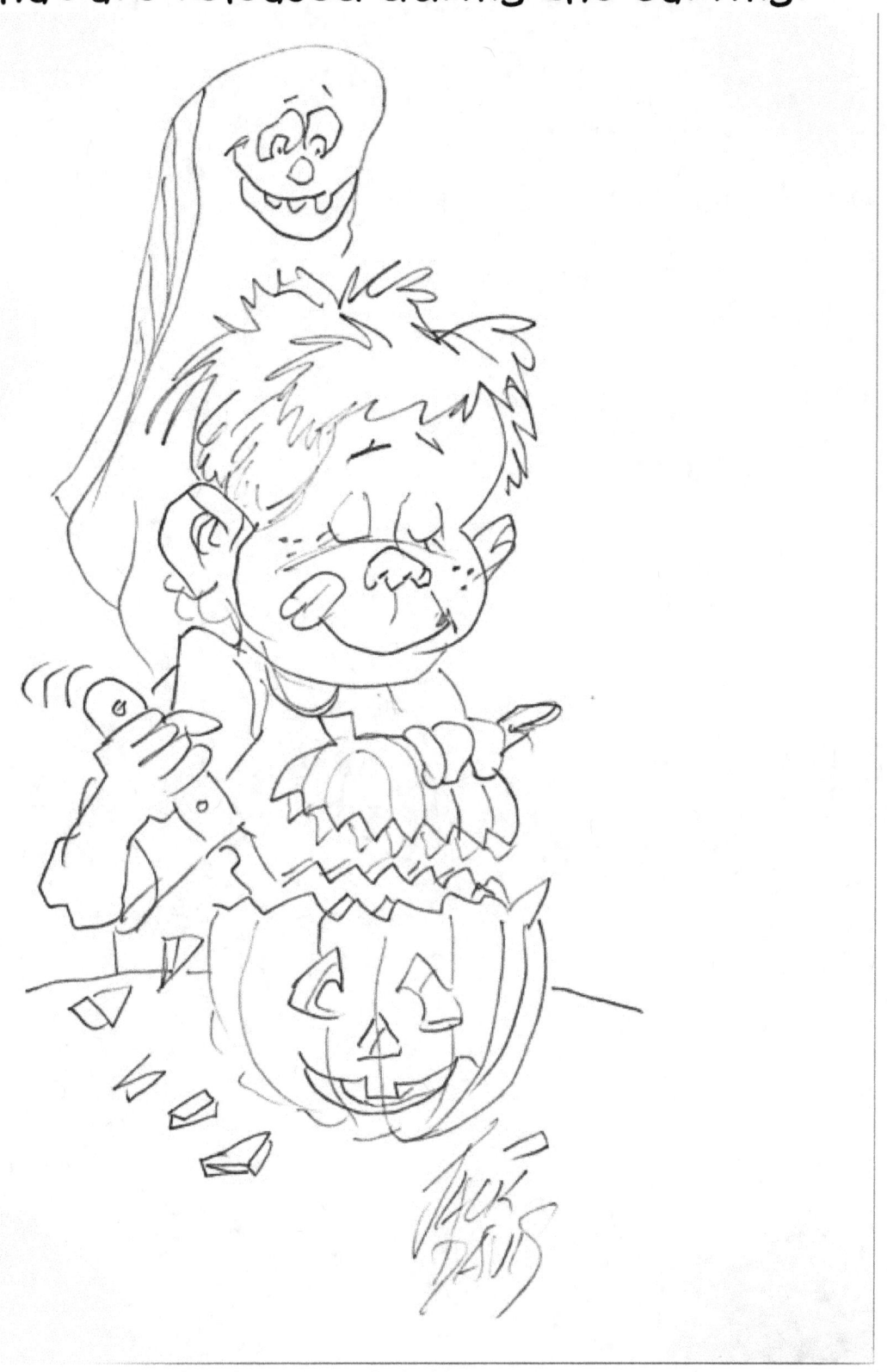

Here we see how young boys who hope to see monsters while trick-or-treating may have to settle for an old witch.

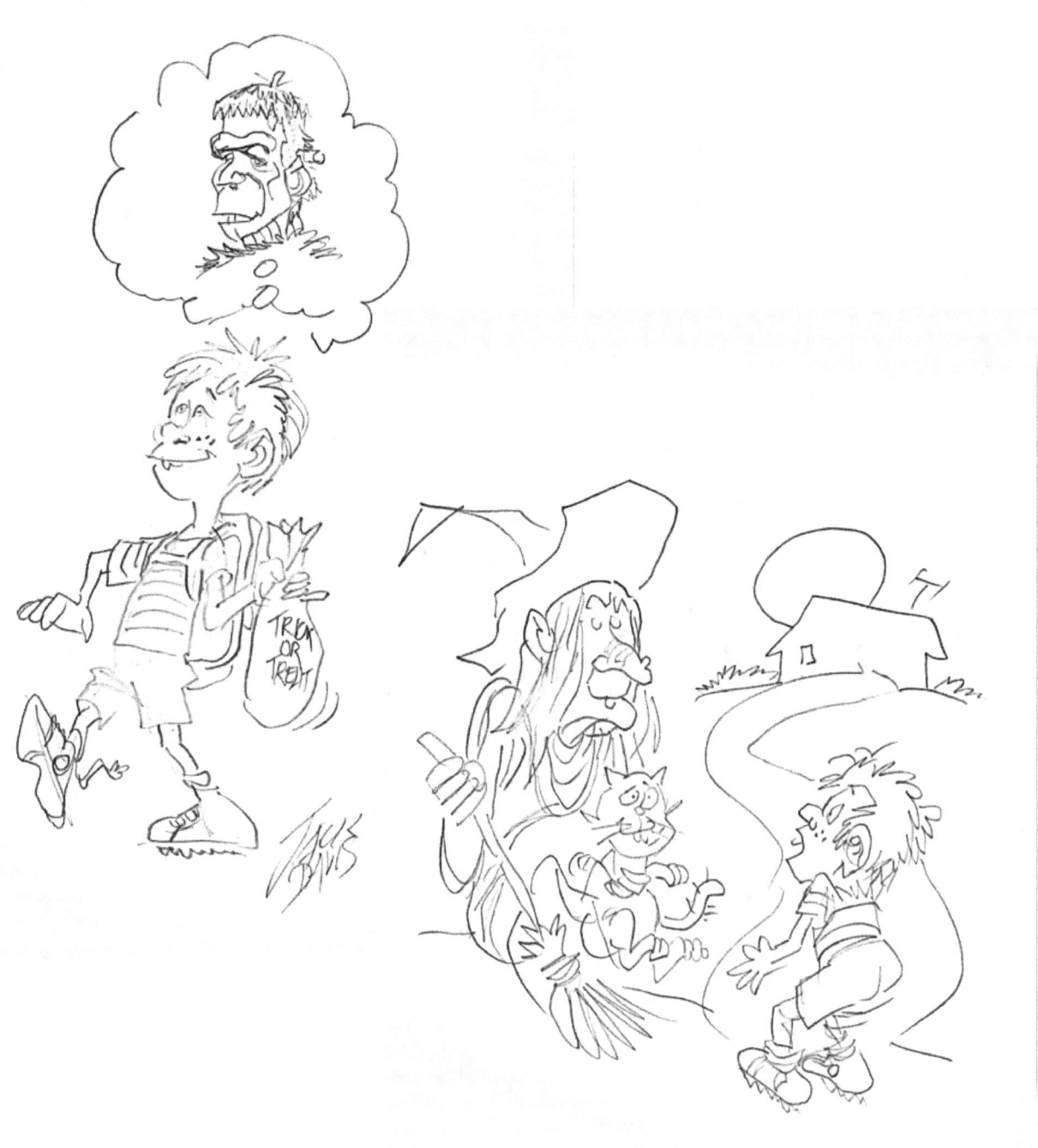

In this sketch we are challenged to guess just how many ideas this young man will envision to celebrate his favorite holiday, Halloween.

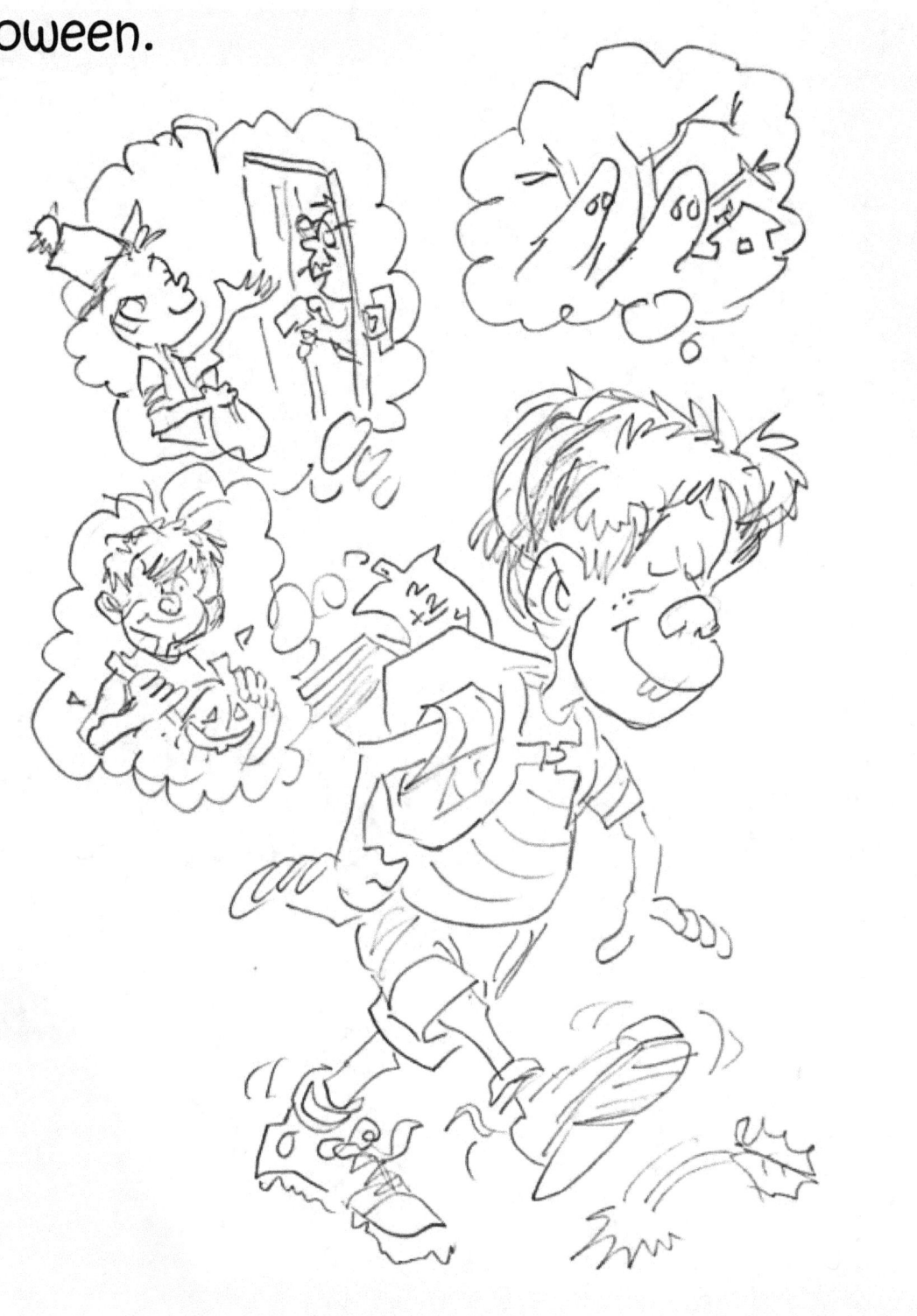

Starting out, Paul would construct simple and innocent Props for Halloween, but over time his creations became more sinister.

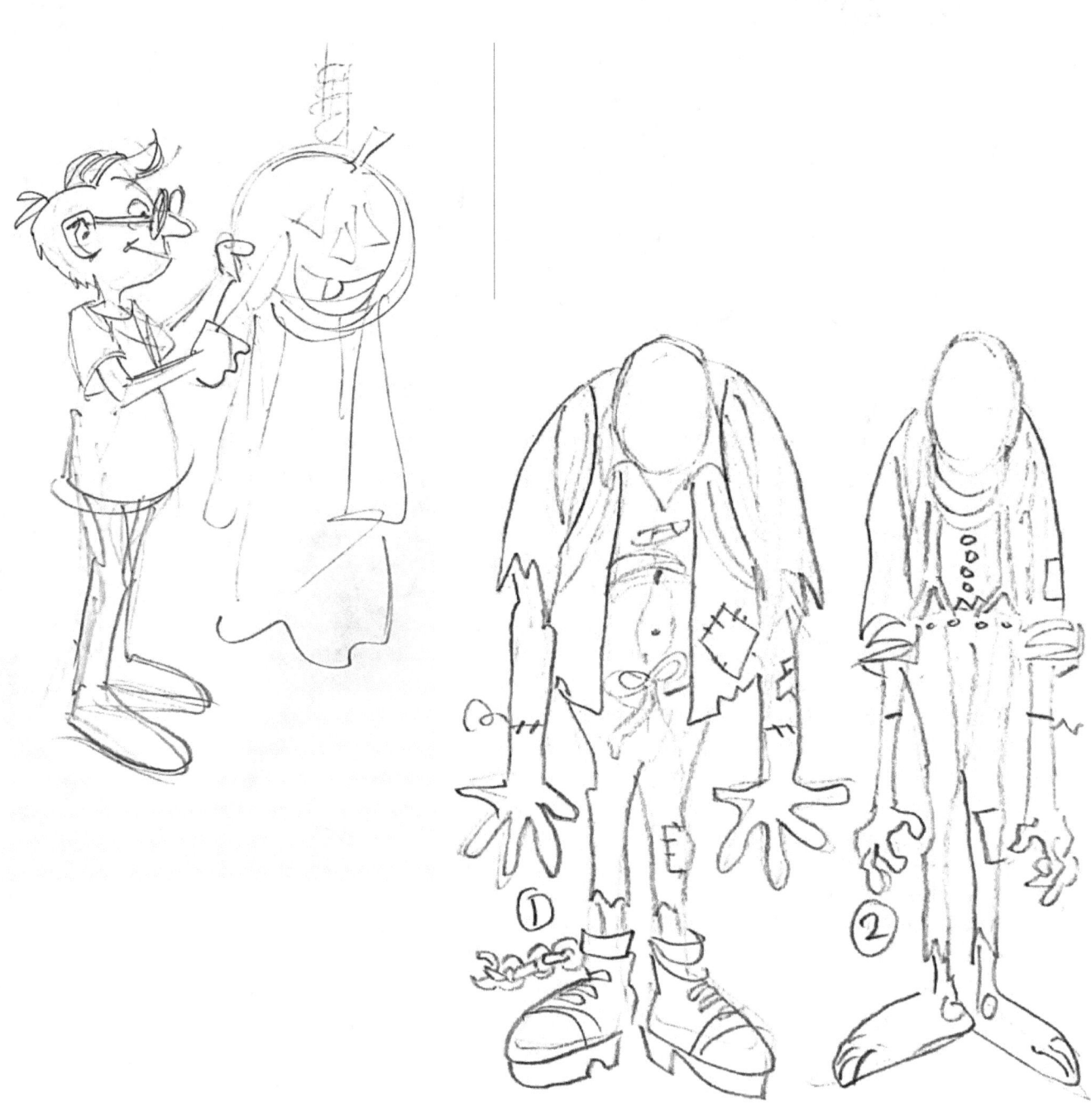

In this sketch we learn a valuable lesson. When the local witch knows you by name it's time to move to another state.

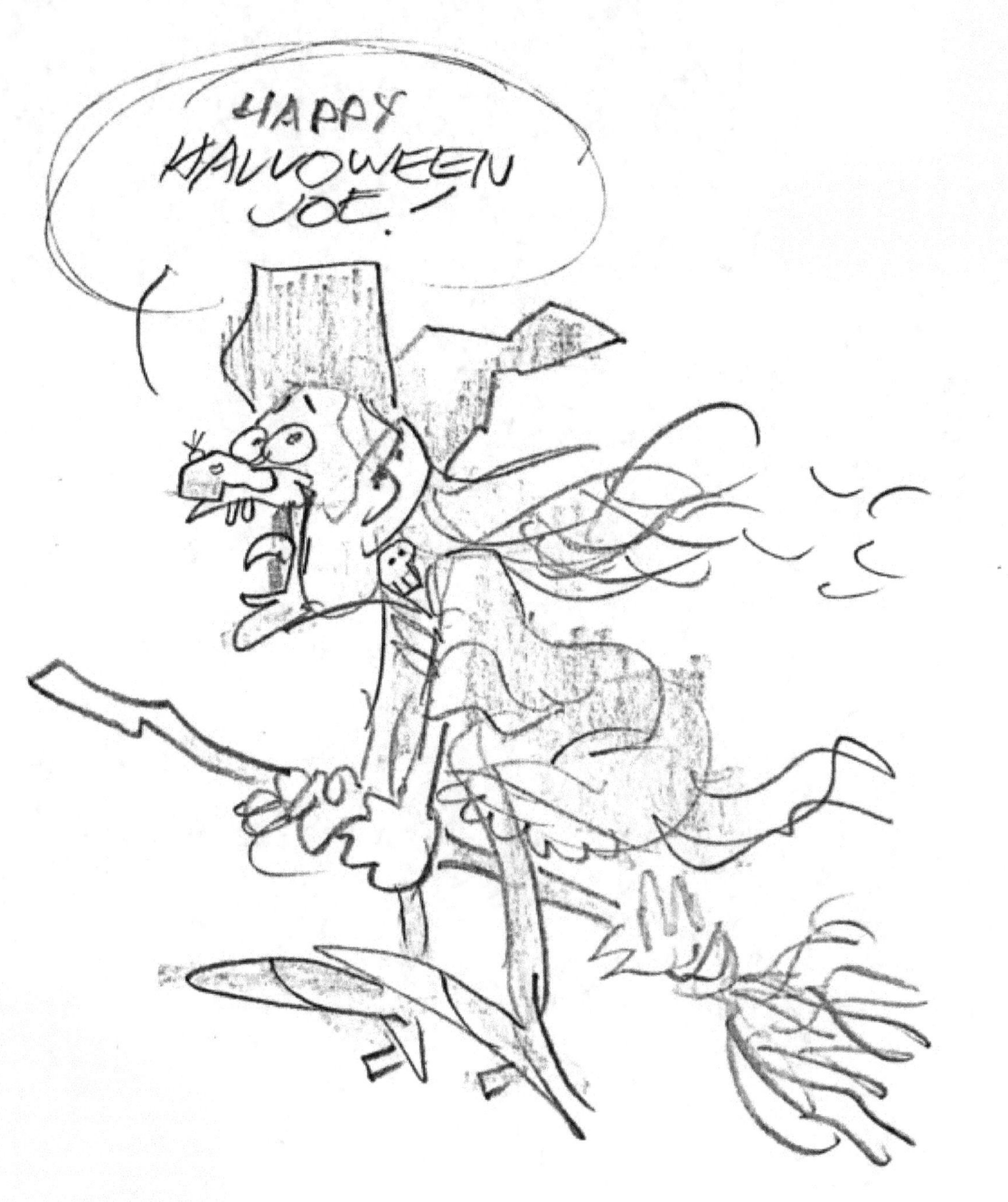

In this sketch we find a headless horseman galloping so fast he seems to be erasing himself.

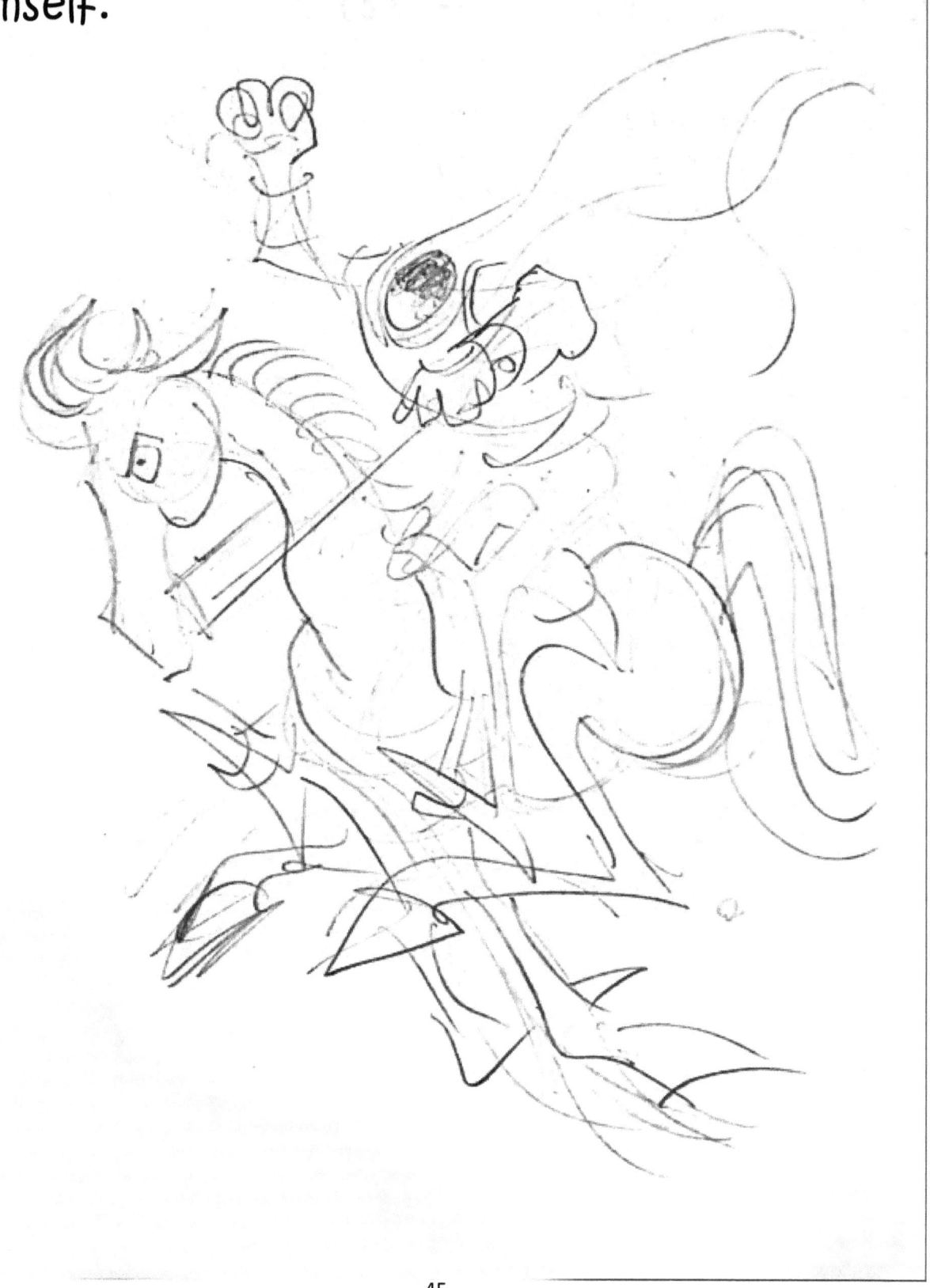

This is a sketch of the author that should have been printed on the back slip jacket.

The artwork is almost as much a mess as is the author.

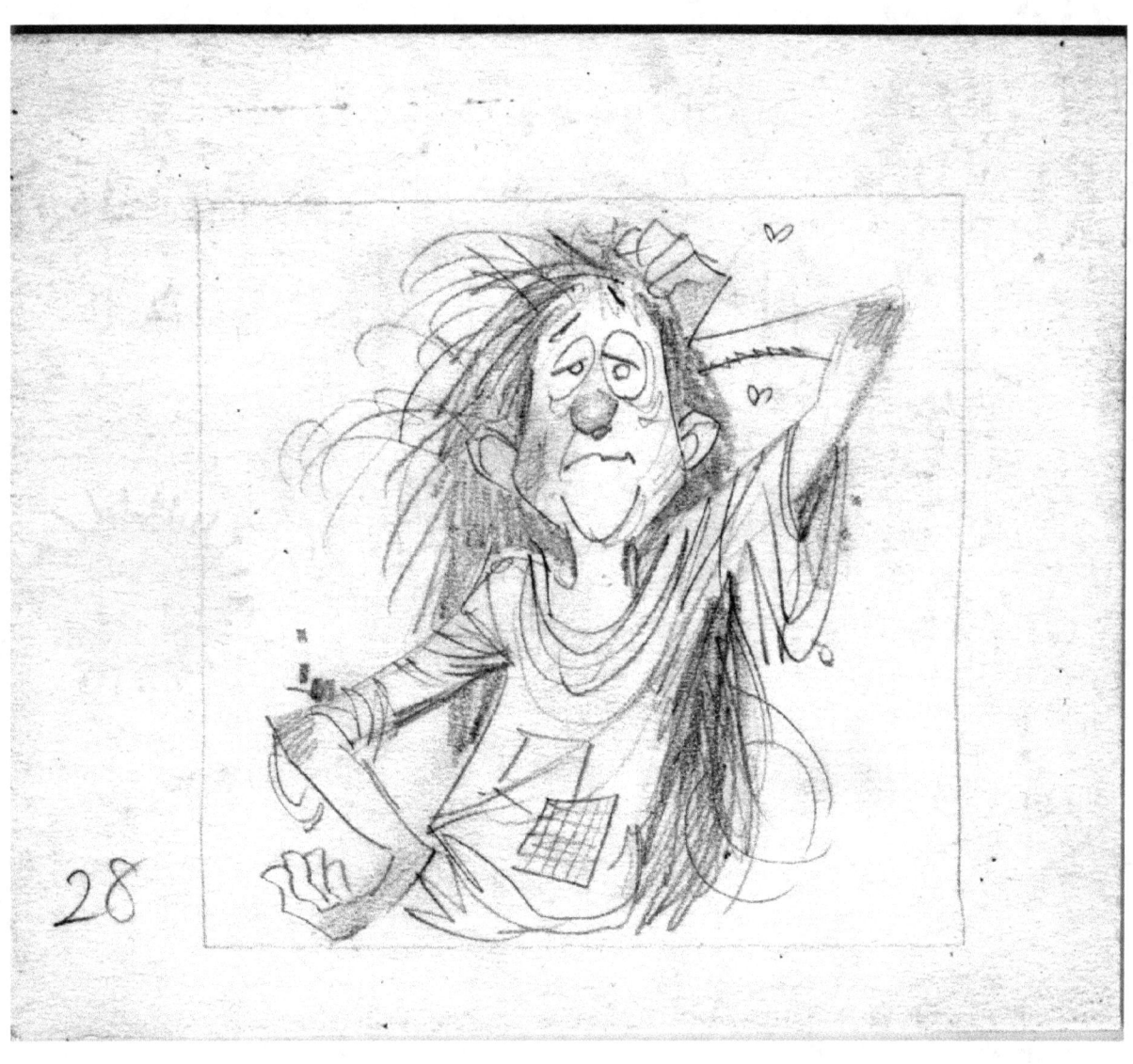

Another valuable lesson to learn from this sketch, hitchhikers should avoid getting rides from a hearse wagon full of ghouls!

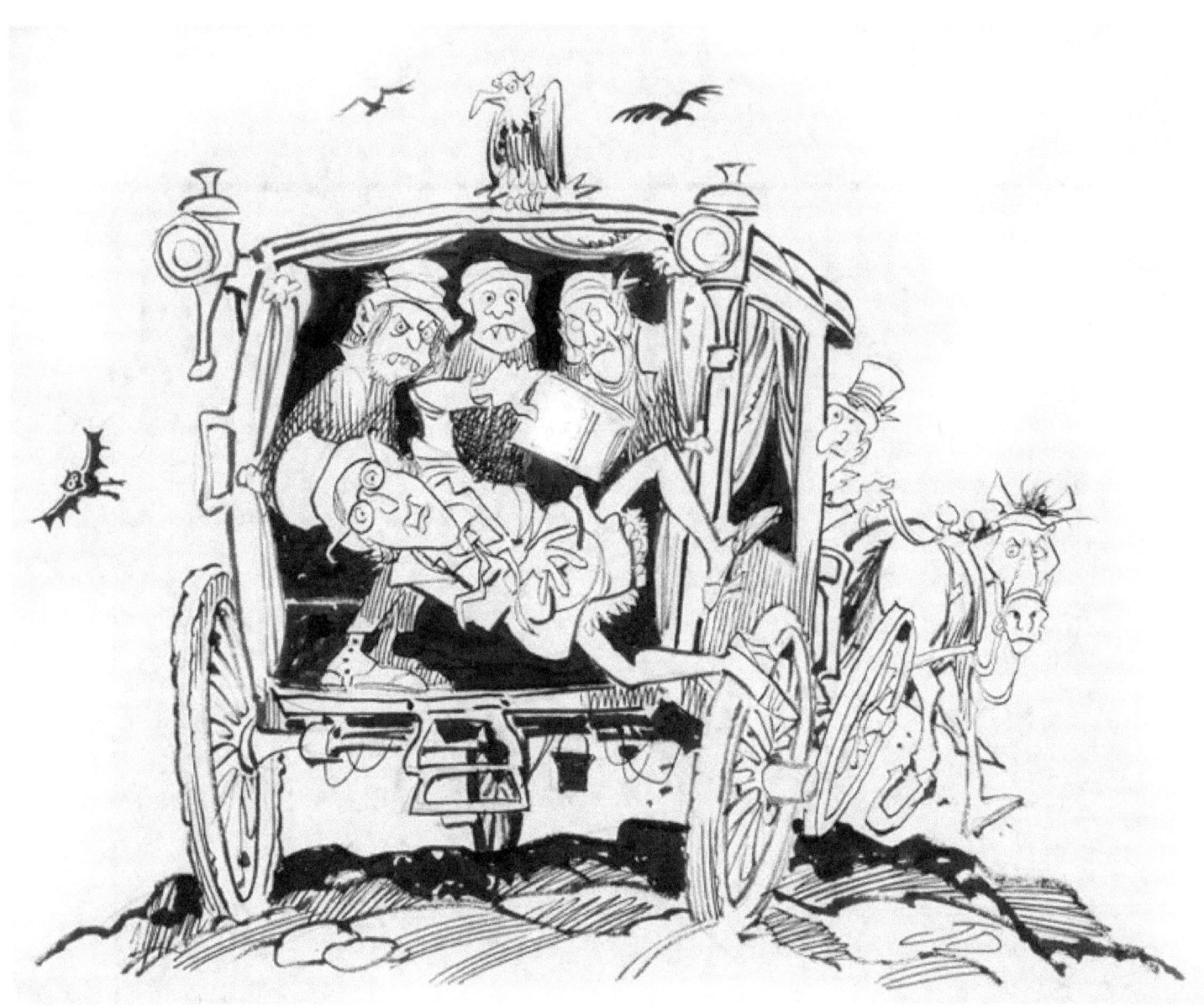

And finally, what was thought to be a quite flower visitation to the cemetery, turned into an evening barbeque hosted by the local inhabitants. Exactly what or who were they cooking can be anyone's guess?

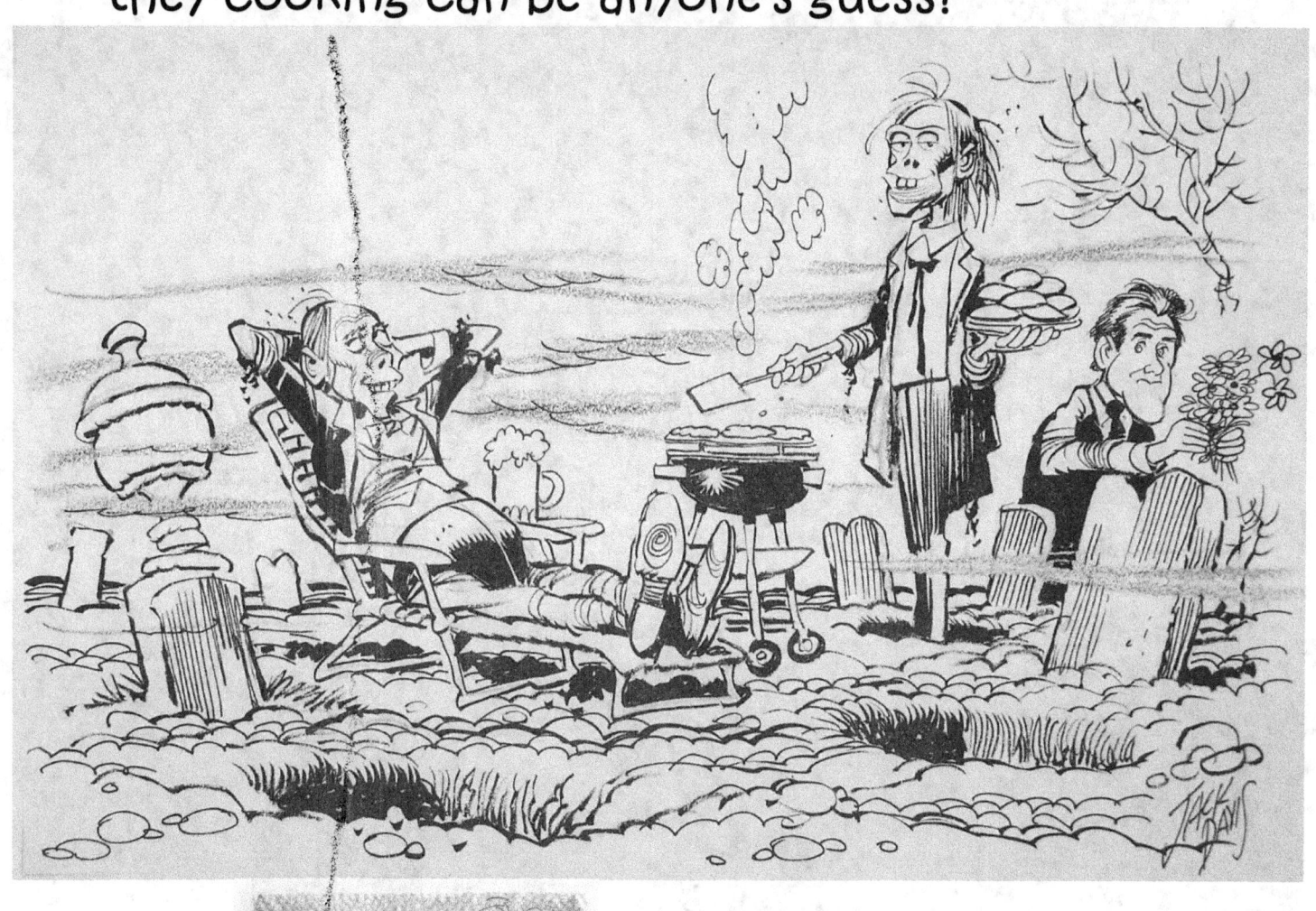

... And if you made it through the entire book, you can join our club.

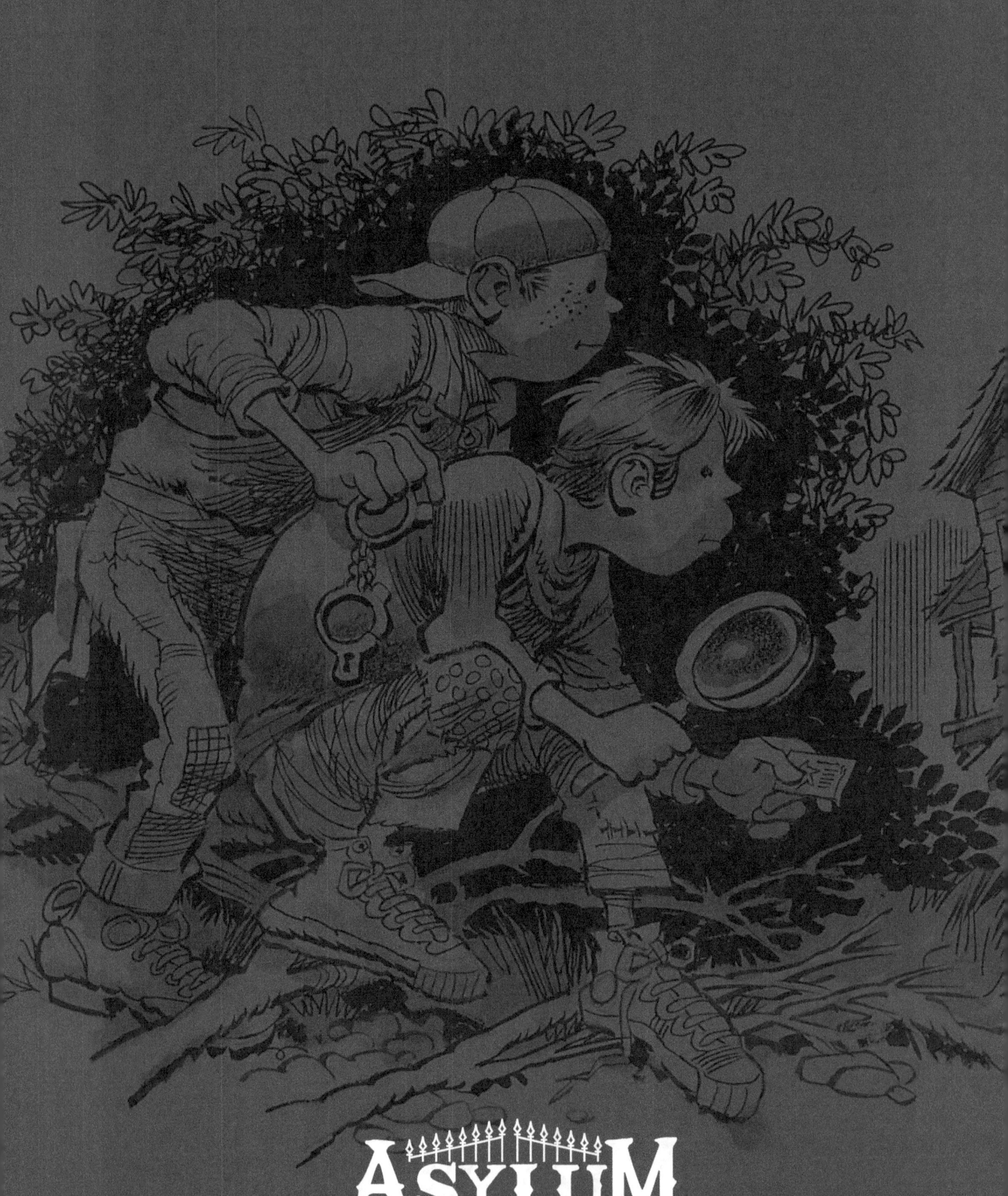

www.ingramcontent.com/pod-product-compliance
Lightning Source LLC
Chambersburg PA
CBHW062343220526
45469CB00008B/2818